My Mom and Dad
on the coast south of
Big Sur

A historical recollection of the Big Sur area experienced through the toils and labor of the Harlan family.

Stanley Harlan

ABOUT THE AUTHOR

Stan Harlan, the youngest of 3 brothers of George and Esther Harlan, was born in San Jose California on November 11, 1927. As with his two older brothers, their mother, Esther, left the coastal family ranch near Lucia on the Big Sur coast, when she was within a week of giving birth, to be with her mother, and the family doctor, Doctor Blanchard, in Campbell, California.

This trip was a difficult two-day journey, First, over narrow mountain trails from the coast to the San Antonio Valley and an Indian Cave on the first day. An overnight stay at the Indian cave was followed by a horse drawn Spring Wagon trip from there to King city on the following day, and then a train trip to San Jose.

The return trip to the coastal ranch came a week after Stan's birth. On the final leg of the trip, over the narrow mountain trails, he was placed in a five-gallon kerosene can, which had one side cut out and lined with blankets, then placed and tied on the pack saddle of George's favorite mule, Big Jack. This is how Stan arrived at the family ranch at Lopez Point, as did his brothers before him.

Stan's mother, Esther, had learned to do all phases of ranch work, in addition to being a mother of three children and a full-time public school teacher at Redwood School. George, at this time, was a federal mail carrier over the mountains from Jolon to the Lucia Post Office; as well as running the family cattle ranch. Stan was her student from grade one through grade eight.

Upon graduation from the eighth grade, Stan postponed high school for one year and helped his father do ranching chores. In 1942, Stan enrolled in Pacific Grove High School and was a graduate there in 1946. He excelled in Industrial Arts, football, math and science.

For fear of being drafted, he joined the U. S. Army paratroopers in San Francisco on October 5, of 1946. World War Two was over and paratroopers were not needed, so he was directed into the occupation forces in Germany after completing Basic Training at Fort Jackson in South Carolina.

His experiences on detachment duty in Germany were many and quite rewarding. He met Irene Marus (a Polish national), his future wife there, in 1947. They were married on March 1, 1948 and lived a rewarding life together until her death on October 5, 2015.

Upon returning from the Service in 1948, Stan worked on the ranch, worked over a year in the timber industry and then registered at The University of California at Santa Barbara in September of 1949. While there he completed the 4-year course in 3 years by taking overloads and Summer sessions. He graduated in August of 1952 with a B. A. Degree and a Special Secondary Teaching Credential in Industrial Arts. Stan and Irene's daughter, Carmen, was born in 1950, while Stan was in attendance at the University.

Upon Graduation from UCSB Stan was hired by the Watsonville High School District as a teacher of Industrial Arts. He completed 32 years of very rewarding work there, until his retirement in 1984. He served a number of years as Department Chairman.

Stan and Irene always were involved in, and connected to, the Harlan Ranch at Lopez Point. Many Summers, holidays and weekends were spent there in helping out with the chores of cattle ranching.

In 1968, Stan and Irene bought an empty lot in Monterey, and over two years, constructed a family home, primarily with their two hands and ingenuity. They moved into their new home in 1970 and have fully enjoyed their mature years there.

Irene, with Stan's assistance, has published four family history books in 1989 and a few years following. Stan has researched and written a number of history books relating to the Big Sur coastal area, the homesteads, the tan bark industry, Redwood School and stories of his experiences on the coastal ranch.

FOREWORD

I chose to write the following about my parents because of the many outstanding hardships that they experienced in making a go of their life on the truly beautiful, but, at the same time, trying, Big Sur South Coast.

My mother and father were true pioneers of the Big Sur South Coast. My father, George Alwin Harlan, was born there on October 22, 1893. He was the third eldest child of Wilber Judson Harlan and Ada Amanda Dani Harlan (Wilber homesteaded and settled in the area in 1885). He was also the grandchild of still another pioneer homesteading family (the Danis, who came to the area in 1876). My mother, Mary Esther Smith, born on the 19th of October 1892, in Campbell, California, was also a granddaughter of 3rd generation pioneers (the Youngs and the Johnsons of the San Jose area).

My father lived his full life of 91 years in this area. He learned the trade of cattle raising well and became an expert in providing the necessary environment for producing high quality beef on this rugged land. He also learned many ranch related skills and practiced the raising of other farm animals and products for market as well. His knowledge of the land and its limitations were foremost in his mind. He practiced the techniques required to raise and harvest the hay and other by products without fault. He always looked to the future in improving the infrastructure of roadways, water spring development and the maintenance of clear grazing land with efficient erosion control. He also knew and practiced the art of game management to a level that most outsiders envied.

My mother, spending her younger years in the city, did not have the same background knowledge of this coastal area. She was a fast learner, however, and the country and the people made her feel that she would like to be a part of it. She came here to teach Redwood School in 1913 as a graduate of the San Jose State Normal School. She boarded at the Harlan home and fell in love with her job and many of the people in the area. One of which, was George Alwin Harlan, the third eldest of the Harlan children. They started a life together in 1916 and began a family in 1921.

I have tried to present an accurate picture of their trials and tribulations over the years, as time passed, and the hard-earned rewards of their labors started to be realized in their later years. Life was not easy for them, but it was never without promise. The sheer physical exhaustion of each day's work left little time or energy for mutual relaxation. I believe that the growth and successes of their three sons in their lifetime endeavors was a tribute to their high ethics, values, a belief in strong disciplinary values, a demonstration of hard work examples and a belief and practice in fairness to others.

It is, with these thoughts in mind, that I have made an attempt to present some, but definitely not all, of their life experiences for others to read.

My Mom and Dad

GEORGE AND ESTHER HARLAN'S WEDDING PICTURE

October 29, 1916

MY MOM AND DAD

I have often wondered how my mother was able to face the many challenges that she experienced as a mother of three sons, a public-school teacher, a housewife to a (ever busy) cattle rancher, an excellent cook, a good housekeeper with extreme restrictions on labor saving conveniences, and still able to achieve so many accomplishments.

Mary Esther Smith, the eldest of four children, was born October 19, 1892, to Lucy Farrell (Young) Smith and Frederick William Smith, in Campbell, Santa Clara County, California. She attended Campbell Public Schools and then went on to complete her teaching credentials at San Jose Normal School (now California State University at San Jose). Upon completion of her college work, in the summer of 1913, she was told of a teaching position at a small country school in the Santa Lucia Mountains, near the Pacific Ocean and west of King City.

She embarked on this new adventure on July 31, 1913, by taking the train to King City with her younger brother, Leonard. At King City she said goodbye to Leonard, who returned to Campbell by train. She then boarded a mail stagecoach toward Jolon that same day, which took her to a branch of the wagon road, called the Big Gate, near the San Antonio Mission. Previously arranged, she was to meet with one of the school board members of Redwood School, Wilber Judson Harlan, at this junction. Everything worked out as planned and Wilber was waiting there with a spring wagon and a two-horse team. Esther, as she was usually called, was concerned that she may not be accepted by the school board to teach at this remote school, but Wilber assured her that they would all be glad to see her take on the job. Wilber helped transfer the luggage from the stage coach to the spring wagon, and they were off to the Mission and points beyond.

It had been a long day and toward evening they came to a natural sandstone cave in the San Antonio River valley that had been used for generations by the Indians and early coastal settlers for overnight shelter. The Spring Wagon was backed by the team of horses up an incline of about 10 feet to the wide opening of the cave. The harnesses were removed and hung from metal hooks which had been secured to the ceiling of the cave to prevent damage by rats and mice. The horses, after being watered in the nearby river bottom, were led up a steep trail to a plateau on top of the cave rocks, where they were released for overnight grazing. The only access to this area was by this trail so, after releasing the horses, it was blocked at the terminus of the plateau. There was a limited quantity of dry grass on this plateau which the horses fed on during the night. The horses were familiar to this regimen because each time one of the family members went to town (King City) they would stop over at this cave to accomplish the two-day trip of 50 miles in each direction.

My mother experienced her first night away from home and with a stranger at that! There were all kinds of experiences, new to her, on that memorable night. Food stuffs and blankets were stored in a large wooden chest that rested on the cave floor. Wilber prepared the evening meal by boiling pieces of potato in a metal can over an open fire. He had brought a few pieces of venison jerky on the trip as well, which they consumed for the evening meal.

Wilber instructed my mother to sleep on an old wagon bed at the rear of the cave, and he slept separately on the ground in a distant corner of the cave. They both slept in their day time clothing. He used a saddle and saddle blankets for a pillow. She used her shoes and a coat for a pillow. Each of them had a single wool blanket for warmth, but at this time of the year the nights were quite warm. There were no lights of any kind at this cave so as night fell total darkness took over. All of the small animals became active and made their traditional noises, none of which my mother was familiar with.

There were wood rats that moved about looking for things they might eat or carry off to their nests. They also were using a communal signal of vibrating their tail against the leaves or any other object they might be resting on. Mice, of course, were regular visitors throughout the night making their rustling noises and occasional squeaking. A skunk came by this night making his traditional "tap-tap"

LUCY FARRELL YOUNG SMITH and FREDERICK WILLIAM SMITH
Parents of Mary Esther Smith Harlan

Lucy was a descendant of Archibald and Mary Little Johnson, early pioneers (1849) of the Santa Clara Valley

MARY ESTHER SMITH LEAVING HER FAMILY HOME IN CAMPBELL,
CALIFORNIA

*She was heading for her teaching assignment at Redwood School in the Santa
Lucia Mountains south of Big Sur in August of 1913.*

MARY ESTHER SMITH'S GRADUATION DIPLOMA FROM CAMPBELL UNION HIGH SCHOOL

Dated June 22,1911

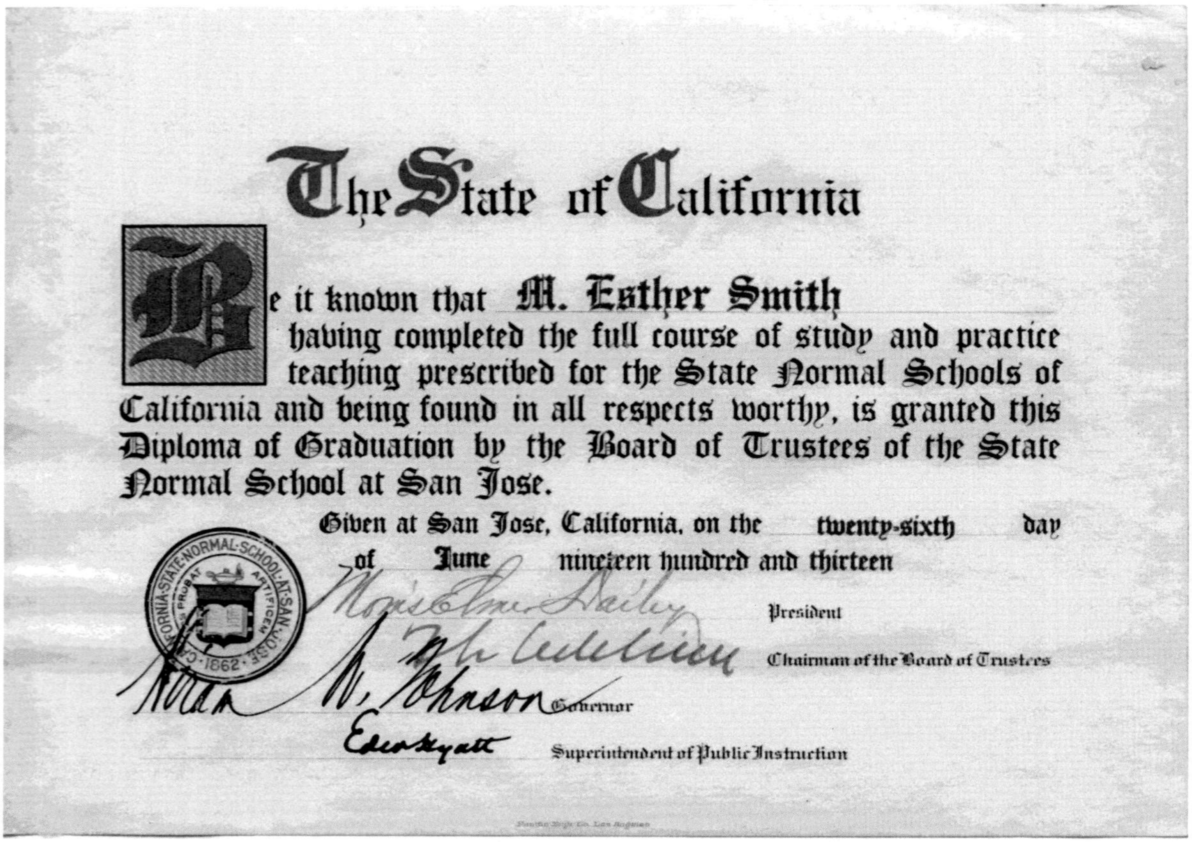

The State of California

Be it known that M. Esther Smith having completed the full course of study and practice teaching prescribed for the State Normal Schools of California and being found in all respects worthy, is granted this Diploma of Graduation by the Board of Trustees of the State Normal School at San Jose.

Given at San Jose, California, on the twenty-sixth day of June nineteen hundred and thirteen

President

Chairman of the Board of Trustees

Governor

Superintendent of Public Instruction

MARY ESTHER SMITH'S GRADUATION DIPLOMA FROM CALIFORNIA NORMAL SCHOOL AT SAN JOSE, CALIFORNIA

Dated June 26, 1913

California State Normal School later became California State University at San Jose

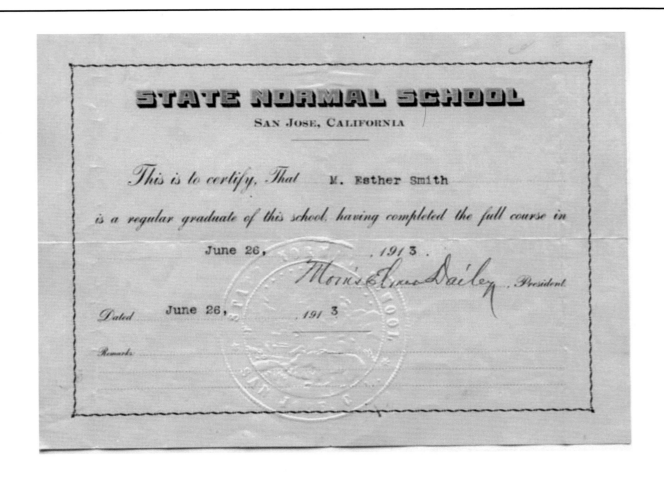

CERTIFICATE OF COMPLETION OF THE COURSES
OFFERED AT SAN JOSE STATE NORMAL SCHOOL
FOR M. ESTHER SMITH

*My mother received this certificate of completion along with her graduation
diploma on June 26, 1913.*

A PORTION OF THE INDIAN CAVE THAT MARY ESTHER SMITH
STAYED IN OVER NIGHT ON HER WAY TO THE COAST WITH
WILBER JUDSON HARLAN IN AUGUST OF 1913

*Note the many mortar holes that were created by the Indians in grinding acorns
from nearby oak trees. This area is in the far-right end of the cave as you would
look into it from the east.*

noises with his feet while checking out the camp fire for any leftover food particles. A great horned owl, perched on a tree limb near the cave entrance, also chimed in with his repetitious hoot, hoot, hoot for most of the night.

My mother wrote of her experiences that night as follows:

> "I removed my shoes and used them and my coat for a pillow. I had a blanket for a cover. It seemed impossible to sleep as it was my first experience at camping out. Rats soon appeared and from all the noise they made, there must have been several rat families represented. I felt safe from rats as I didn't think they could get up over the wagon wheels.
>
> The real fright came later. Toward morning I heard 'pitter-patter,' 'pitter-patter', and the first thing that entered my mind was--a bear! a lion! After what appeared to be ages, I decided to call out if I heard the noise again. I 'hated' to appear as a tenderfoot so time and again I refrained from calling out. I was almost a nervous wreck, before the noise ceased, at the approach of daylight. When I told Mr. Judson[1] what I had heard, he informed me that it was either a skunk or a coyote."

After a hurried breakfast of boiled potatoes and jerky, Wilber retrieved the horses from the plateau above the cave. He saddled them and loaded on my mother's belongings. He checked to make sure the fire was safe and all of the material goods were safely stored.

The wagon road ended at the cave location and it was necessary to follow a narrow mountain trail the rest of the way to the coast. This trail followed the east side of the San Antonio River for about two miles. Then at a crossing between two massive rocks, called the "Dardanelle's," the trail abruptly started a steep incline to broach the eastern slopes of the Santa Lucia Mountain Range.

The day became very warm and the horses perspired heavily climbing the steep trail called the Carrizo Springs Trail. At one point on this trail one could see the Sipriano Avila home which was called the "*Salsipuedes Rancho*" to the left and somewhat below the vantage point. Continuing on up the hill they eventually came to the Carrizo Springs, which, on a hot day, would seem like paradise. My mother wrote,

> "Never was a drink of water more welcome than that one was. The spring was large and looked so cool and refreshing. There were enormous brakes (ferns) back of the spring and several large trees were nearby. One laurel tree was

---

[1] Mr. Judson was Wilber Judson Harlan

very large. There were several improvised stoves close by so I knew it must be
a favored camping site."

Refreshed from the cool air under the trees and the fresh spring water both people
and horses were ready to continue the climb toward the top of the mountain. The
trail was not quite as steep as it had been earlier, and it followed a route more on
the northerly face of the slope. There were more large trees, including Sugar Pines
and Santa Lucia Firs, which created some shade to those on the trail. Also, along
this part of the trail, there were extremely large boulders and outcroppings of
sandstone. Some of these had weather worn holes and even small caves indicating
they had once been in a stream bed or at a sea shore. My mother was very
impressed by these sights and frequently quizzed Wilber about how he thought
these things may have been formed. Wilber, a self-taught student of nature, had
very plausible answers to her questions that might parallel those of the most
sophisticated university professors.

Continuing on up the trail they eventually intersected the Coast Ridge Trail, which
was very near the top of the mountain and at about 4,000 feet elevation. It was
here that the trail leveled off considerably, and in a few minutes they were at the
intersection of the Gamboa Trail which would eventually lead them down to the
Harlan homestead. In 1913, the Gamboa Trail extended for a quite a distance
through rocky brush land toward the ridge separating the Canogas and Cuevas
forks of Big Creek. It then descended sharply down the southerly side of this ridge,
which had some grass land on it, to a point where it crossed the Canogas Fork a
few hundred yards upstream from the present-day Ojito camp. Upon crossing the
creek, the trail again rose sharply out of the canyon bottom to the Ojito Gap
between the Big Creek and Lime Kiln drainage. My mother often referred to this
trail as being very extreme in both steepness and beauty. In places it was difficult
to stay in the saddle, and it was always necessary to tighten the cinches on the
horse's saddles before embarking on these slopes. In other places one could look
horizontally at the tops of tall trees only a few feet away with their trunks
somewhere below clinging to the steep and rocky cliff faces. Horses not trained to
navigate these extremes would probably not survive very long without falling to
their death.

Upon reaching the Ojito Gap; the trail continued for nearly a mile in a south
westerly direction, and nearly level, to a point which was called the Big Oak.
There was an extremely large Valpariso oak at this location with a split redwood
picket fence coral under its spreading limbs. The Gamboa Trail made a turn to the
right and another trail continued on in a southerly direction. The horses knew they
were to take the southerly fork and needed no reining to achieve this end. Nearly a

MASSIVE SANDSTONE WALL FORMING WHAT WAS KNOWN AS
THE DARDINELLS

This location is where the Carrizo Trail crossed the river

BOULDERED TRAIL BED OF THE CARRIZO SPRINGS TRAIL

Typical of much of the Carrizo Trail and steep uphill also

AN OLD ENAMELED STEEL SIGN AT CARRIZO SPRING

This area of the Santa Lucia Mountains was once known as the Santa Barbara National Forest. In recent times it is known as the Los Padres National Forest.

EXTREME EROSION OF SANDSTONE BOULDERS AT TRAILSIDE

EXAMPLES OF THE BEAUTIFUL SUGAR PINE ON THE LEFT
AND THE CONICAL SANTA LUCIA FIR ON THE RIGHT

mile further down the mountain the trail forked again near an outcropping of blue soapstone. To the left was the Pine Ridge Trail leading to the Dani homestead, and nearly straight ahead was the trail leading to the Harlan homestead. Again, the horses needed no direction. They knew where rest and feed were located.

About a half hour later the view down to the Pacific would have been observed except for this 1st day in August 1913, there was a blanket of fog at the lower elevations (typical at this time of year). The fog appears as an ocean in itself except for the uneven surface with fingers running up into the redwood canyons.

The trail continued on downward toward the fog layer, but there were many sights to observe adjacent to the trail. There were moderately sloping hills with some open grass lands and many pines and live oak trees. Soon there were small canyons with redwoods, maple, madrone, laurel, and lilac trees. The school that Esther was to teach for many years was located on the right, but since it was getting late in the afternoon, Wilber chose to go right on by.

Another steep downhill run of the trail through lilacs, grease woods, skunk berry (cascara) bushes, and many other varieties of short brush soon brought them within view of their destination. Below them, at the base of a side hill of open grassland, stood a red and white, well built, two story structure of the Harlan family.

Wilber had acquired a Muhly sawmill in the late 1800s which was operated by water power. After an arduous transport of the heavy equipment over the mountain, he established this sawmill on his homestead near some very large redwoods. By digging a half-mile long trench to another stream, he was able to combine the flow of two streams to operate his sawmill during winter months. Over a period of about three winters, he was able to produce enough lumber for the construction of this large home for his family in 1900.

Esther was to board with the Harlan's during her tenure as teacher at Redwood School. Very weary and saddle sore, Esther dismounted from the horse, hardly able to stand, near the front gate of the Harlan homestead house. She was greeted shyly by a number of the ten Harlan children who ranged in age from five to twenty-two years. The elder boys were not at home, but Lulu May, about the same age as Esther, greeted her graciously with open arms. Mrs. Ada Amanda Dani Harlan, Wilber's wife and the children's mother also greeted her very openly.

Lulu helped unload Esther's belongings and took her upstairs to a very nicely decorated room with a small veranda. Lulu helped Esther unpack her belongings and showed Esther where she could freshen up. Lulu and Mrs. Harlan then invited Esther into the large kitchen-dining room for a hearty evening meal. Esther and the rest of the family sat at the long family table, and Esther related how impressed she was of her trip over the Santa Lucias. As she and the older folks ate, the younger children sat on the far side staring at her. Esther was somewhat disturbed and self-conscious by this experience, but graciousness of the rest of the family soon put her at ease. Esther was very tired after the two days of travel so she retired soon after dinner.

The next morning, she felt stiff but much less tired. After breakfast, she asked if she could look at the school house she was to teach in, and it was agreed that Marion David Harlan, only five years old, was to go along with her to show her the way. The Harlan home was about 800 feet elevation and the school house was very near 1680 feet elevation. The trail leading to the school was understandably steep and crossed one fairly large canyon. There were beautiful redwoods in the canyon and a large outcropping of rock near the school itself. It did not take long to get to school as Marion moved along very quickly.

Esther was very positively impressed with her first view of the school. It was small but very neat and was painted white. Upon entering it, she found nice blackboards, neatly arranged desks in good condition, an organ, a phonograph and two library sections stocked with very good books. Time passed quickly and she and Marion were to return to the Harlan house for lunch.

After lunch, she suggested that she return to school and make preparations for opening day on Monday. Wilber suggested she ride their mule to the school house since she was still stiff from her travel over the mountain. In short order, he saddled the mule and tied him near the front gate. Esther climbed aboard and the two of them headed up the hill to the school. The mule traveled very slowly, recognizing there was an inexperienced rider on his back. They did arrive at the school without miss-hap and Esther worked a few hours getting everything ready for the students. Returning down the hill that afternoon, the mule traveled more slowly than he had going up the hill. So much so that Mr. and Mrs. Harlan, who were observing from the house, called out and asked what might be wrong with the mule. It was obvious the mule was taking advantage of a good thing and not overworking himself.

The next day, on Sunday, Esther had been invited over to a neighbor and former teacher of Redwood School in 1905-1906 and 1907-1908 school years. Her name was Mrs. Bertha Janes Lopez, who had also gone to San Jose Normal School a few

THE WILBER HARLAN HOME AS IT LOOKED IN 1913

As Mary Esther Smith approached the Harlan home from the mountain side in the background this is what she saw.

years before Esther. They had known each other in Campbell, so it was a pleasant experience to meet and discuss their common teaching vocations. Bertha had married Anicetto Mariano Lopez, the eldest son of Agapito Manuel Lopez and Angustia Romero Lopez (one of the first homestead families in the area), at the end of her first year of teaching at Redwood School. The Lopez homestead was only a half-mile west of the Harlan home at about the same elevation.

Esther enjoyed her visit with the Lopez family on that Sunday, August 3, 1913. She talked at length with Bertha, and it helped greatly in preventing Esther from becoming homesick. Bertha also gave Esther a number of pointers about teaching at Redwood School, since Bertha had taught there two separate years before. Esther returned to the Harlan home in plenty of time to make the final preparations for the start of school the next day.

Esther, the new teacher of Redwood School, arrived at the school house early so she would be there before the children arrived. She was surprised to find six Spanish and three white children waiting for her on top of the School House Rock. There were also five children of the Harlan family accompanying her to school as well. Some of the other homestead families, who lived in the area, were Borondas, Avilas, Cosios, Danis, Gamboas, Swendings and Twitchels, to name a few. Esther noticed one of the students of Spanish heritage was extremely large. That would have been Peter Cosio who was taller than Esther and weighed over two hundred pounds. Others of Spanish heritage would have been Julia Ancaletta Lopez, Adelina Avila, Bennie Avila, Ben Boronda, Browlia Boronda, Manuela Boronda and Sussie Boronda. Those of whiter skin would have been Carl Paulson Swending, Hannah Christina Twitchel, Bessie Inez Twitchel and Marjorie Ellen Twitchel. Those of the Harlan family that accompanied her to school would have been Ada Alice Harlan, Albert Victor Harlan, Frederick Levi Harlan, Hester Elizabeth Harlan and Marion David Harlan.

The new teacher, at her first job, thoroughly enjoyed her teaching experiences that first year, though the pay was limited, and the students were spread from the first through the seventh grades. She said, "All of the children were good children and although, I had many grades, I enjoyed the work very much". Her stay with the Harlans was also very pleasant, and she began to love the country.

An extended winter vacation was allowed, since the school year started early in the fall. Esther returned to her home in Campbell over the holidays and then attended an institute session (which was typical of all county teachers at that time) before returning to Redwood School in the spring.

19

Official county records indicated, for the school year 1913-1914, the State apportionment for the school was $352.50 and county funds contributed $430.00 for a total of $782.50. A negative balance from the previous year left $629.39 for the full year. Of that sum $560.15 was paid to Esther for her salary. $29.81 was spent for books and $16.01 for contingencies such as firewood, etc. A carry over of $23.42 was left available for the next school year. There were 786 volumes in the school library. The school building was valued at $500.00, the library at $500.00 and the school apparatus (stove, desks, blackboards, organ, etc) at $50.00.

Esther continued teaching at Redwood School for three full school years through June of 1916. She had become very fond of the country and the people. One of the Harlan young men took her special interest and on October 29, 1916, she married George Alwin Harlan, the third eldest of the Harlan family. Neither of them had accumulated much wealth except a few dollars that Esther saved from her three years of teaching and similarly a few more dollars that George had saved from raising a few head of livestock and doing odd jobs in the area. George and the older Harlan boys also worked in the Salinas Valley on the grain threshing machines to earn a few extra dollars. These jobs were quite dangerous and George's grandfather, Gabriel Dani, lost an arm to the threshing machines. The work was very difficult, and the weather was usually very hot at the time of the year when the grain was being threshed.

George was the third child born to Wilber Judson Harlan and Ada Amanda Dani Harlan on October 22, 1893. He greeted this world at the Dani Place, just a mile away from where his parent's homestead was located. His grandmother, Elizabeth Brown Dani, served as mid-wife to many of the young mothers in the area. At the time of his birth, George and the other four members of the family lived in the original homestead cabin that Wilber Harlan had built in 1885. It was called the "Old House" located in section 17. Like all of the Harlan children, George grew up with an affinity to hard work and long hours. Usually barefoot, he attended Redwood School through the seventh grade and graduation. His father, Wilber, paid him a nickel for each gopher or ground squirrel that he caught on the property. He was encouraged to burn brush, and especially wood rat's nests, in the winter and spring months when there was no danger of a fire causing problems.

Wilber also encouraged his children to clear brush and create grasslands. He would get each of his boys started with a few pigs which they cared for diligently until piglets were born. Each boy cleared enough land to plant barley in the spring and upon maturity in the summer gave food for the new crop of pigs. The pigs

A VIEW OF REDWOOD SCHOOL AS IT APPEARED IN 1913
TO STUDENTS APPROACHING FROM THE LOPEZ HOMESTEAD

It was situated on a natural bench on the mountain side nearly a half mile from the Harlan home and at a much higher elevation. Homestead families lived as many as three miles away from the school and their children traveled on narrow mountain trails to reach this remote school. It was built by Wilber Harlan and Chris McQuay in the late 1800's. Some of the timbers were whip sawed from local redwood logs by hand and other materials were milled on Wilber's water powered Muhly saw mill.

The structure replaced a log school building built by Gabriel Dani, Wilber's father-in-law, in 1889.

A CLASS OF REDWOOD SCHOOL STUDENTS WITH TEACHER
BELIEVED TO BE IRENE PARNELL
1909-1910 SCHOOL YEAR

*Irene taught the 1909-1910 school year and again in the fall of the 1910-1911
school year. There are a number of Harlan children in the picture: George just to
the left of the teacher and Paul to the right of the teacher. Lewis Cosio is the
heavy-set student with James Harlan on his shoulders. Aaron Harlan is at far left
and Hester Harlan at far right.*

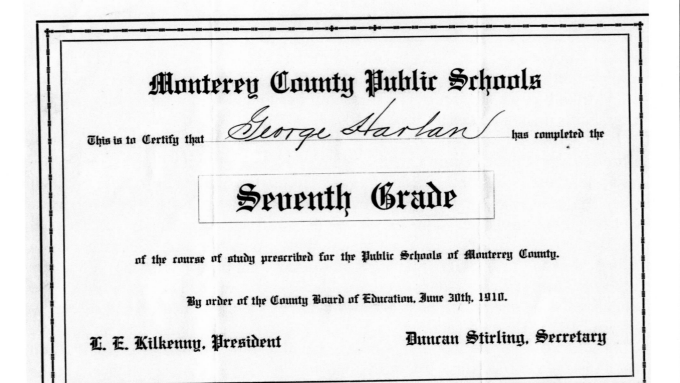

Monterey County Public Schools

This is to Certify that *George Harlan* has completed the

Seventh Grade

of the course of study prescribed for the Public Schools of Monterey County.

By order of the County Board of Education, June 30th, 1910.

L. E. Kilkenny, President   Duncan Stirling, Secretary

A PHOTOCOPY OF GEORGE HARLAN'S 7TH GRADE
GRADUATION CERTIFICATE FROM REDWOOD SCHOOL

George did not go farther than the 7th grade in his formal education, but, for the time, it was considered to be a completion of the elementary grades. His understanding of math, science and geography was more than adequate for his life's endeavors. He was able to survey his land with his own transit and construct any building to minute measurements or ranch road with a high degree of engineering. He understood potential erosion circumstances and made corrections accordingly. He was always eager to learn and readily made changes to make life easier.

were collectively pastured on fallen acorns in the fall, then they were driven on a seven-day arduous trip to King City over the mountain trails for sale in late fall. This gave each of the Harlan sons a "start" in life as they were allowed to keep the profits of the sale of their pigs. George also made a few dollars as a teenager cutting wood for Redwood School. He shared the ranch chores of his parents as well. Milking cows, scything hay, thrashing beans and tilling the family gardens and orchards were a few examples.

Before George's father came to the coast he had worked with Phillip Smith in a nursery in Santa Cruz for a period of time. He learned many skills there on plant husbandry, which he applied to his coastal properties later in life. He worked at the lime kilns in Lime Kiln Creek when he first came to the coast as a homesteader. He cut wood for the furnaces and also managed a team of horses in hauling the wood to the kiln site. My grandfather told me that he worked for fifty cents a day and the work days were 10 hours long in the summer months. He rationalized what seemed to be a low pay scale by saying, "but, I could by a new shirt for 50¢". He said one reason for the kilns to cease operations in the late 1880's was because the wood supply was running out and had to be hauled too great a distance to the kilns. The limestone was in abundant supply adjacent to the kilns and seemed to be no problem in "charging" the kilns with stone.

There were other problems contributing to the closure also. Other lime operations were producing more slacked lime for the cement business than the demands called for and the ownership of the kilns at Lime Kiln Creek changed hands. The Rockland Lime and Cement Company sold out to Henry Cowell Lime and Cement Company. My father said the last load of lime that was shipped out from Rockland Landing became wet in the hold due to rough weather and the load was lost.

With few resources, except love for the land and much hard labor, George and Esther leased a small ranch near Dolan Creek, called the Demas Place. This ranch had a cabin, a barn and a few outbuildings, all made of split redwood lumber that was made from logs that were located in an adjacent canyon called Lime Gulch. They moved there with a few head of cattle, a couple of horses, a 22 rifle and a 410-gauge shotgun. It was especially difficult for them that first year because it was too late to plant a garden, there was no running water at the house and there were no neighbors nearby. The Harlan and Dani families helped them with canned fruit and fresh vegetables when they could make the ten-mile trip by mountain trails to see one another. Lulu was a lifelong friend of Esther from the first day they met.

STEAM POWERED THRESHING MACHINE

This was the type of machine that was in common use in the late 1800's and the early 1900's in the Salinas valley. It was located at a central point in the grain field and the bundles of cut grain stalks were delivered to it in a horse drawn wagon. Many people were employed to keep the machine operating. One fed fuel (probably straw waste) to the fire of the boiler. Another kept the steam engine operating at the proper speed and also made sure water was supplied to the boiler. At least two men fed bundles into the threshing mechanism. One was responsible to sew the filled gunny sacks and another to keep the threshed straw clear of the machine. Two or three crews of men were kept busy bringing the bundles to the thresher. Nearly all of the mature men on the coast took the opportunity to work on the threshing crews in the hot summer months to make spending money. My great grandfather, Gabriel Dani, lost his arm to a threshing machine. It was extremely hot, uncomfortable and dangerous work.

GEORGE ALWIN HARLAN AS A YOUNG MAN

This photo was taken of George before he married Mary Esther Smith.

WILBER JUDSON HARLAN AND ADA AMANDA DANI HARLAN ON
THEIR WEDDING DAY
JULY 7, 1889

George Alwin Harlan's mother and father were married July 7, 1889 in Santa Cruz, California. Wilber came to the Big Sur coast in 1885 and homesteaded land next to the Dani homestead. Ada came to the area with her parents in 1876 as a young girl.

WILBER JUDSON HARLAN'S HOMESTEAD CABIN

Wilber and Ada Harlan lived in this small cabin from 1889 until 1900, when they moved into their new home that Wilber built. Their first six children lived in this house as well. George, the third child born to Wilber and Ada, lived his first seven years in this house.

Solutions to the difficult way of life were gradually met by hard work and ingenuity. Esther would load all of their dirty clothes behind the saddle on one of the horses, and she would ride about a mile to Slates Hot Springs which was also nearly 1,000 feet lower in elevation. There she took advantage of the very hot water (210 degrees F. I have been told) diluted with cold water to achieve the proper washing temperature to wash the clothes by hand on a scrub board. After washing and rinsing she would then repack the wet clothes on the horse and return home to hang them on a line for drying.

Packing fresh water quite a distance to the house from the nearest spring was a painstaking chore every day for both George and Esther. They chose to take some of their hard-earned savings to purchase a ram and about 800 feet of water pipe (which was landed by a fishing boat on the beach and hauled up the hill by horse back). George installed the ram on the bottom of Lime Gulch and supplied it with water from upstream. The ram operated via two different sized valves (a large diameter low pressure one, which, with sufficient volume of water, would force the smaller one to move and force the water in it to a higher elevation). This proved to be quite an experiment and the first real plumbing experience for both of them. The system did work with very little room for error. It required frequent maintenance in replacing the leather valve seats that tended to wear out frequently due to the pounding action of the device. It made it possible for Esther to grow her own garden the following year, however, and she was quite an expert with plants.

George cleared more ground for pasture land and the growing of oat hay. He also cleared brush land by burning in the late fall and then planting the area to barley. This burned over land would grow a vigorous crop of barley just from the winter and spring rains and the very rich soil created by the ash. Part of the crop would be harvested with a scythe when it started to dry in the summer and would be brought into the barn or other buildings for use as chicken feed. The rest of the crop would be left standing and the pigs would be allowed to enter the area for feeding. The oat hay was isolated from the stock for a longer period of time until the "milk" in the grain heads solidified. It would then be cut with a scythe near the ground by hand. A few days later it was gathered into shocks for curing, then, after a couple of more weeks, it was hauled to the barn on a sled for use during the lean days of fall and winter to keep the cattle and horses from getting too weak.

Though the cows that George and Esther had were primarily beef breeds, there were always a few head that were good on milk production. George would "break" a cow to milking after her calf was born in the early spring, by letting the calf nurse the left side while he milked the right side. This "breaking in" would

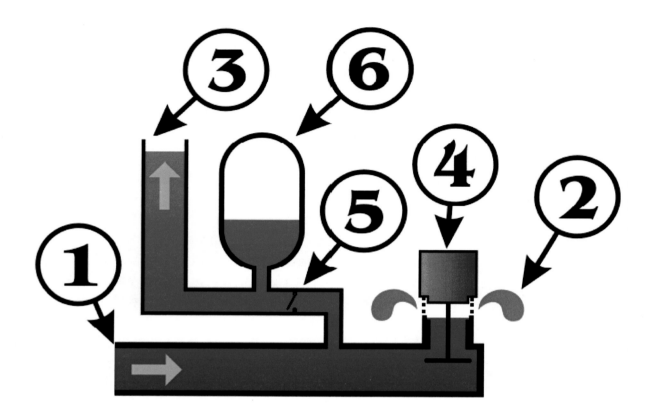

THE WORKINGS OF A HYDRAULIC WATER RAM
(Sketch acquired from the Internet—Wikipedia)

Low pressure, but high volume, water enters at point 1. It freely flows to point 2 through open valve. As the rush of water increases it causes the weight on valve 4 stem to be overcome, thereby closing the valve at point 2. This abruptly causes kinetic energy buildup in the large pipe, thereby forcing a smaller amount of water at a higher pressure through valve 5 to high pressure line 3. As the pressure decreases valve 5 closes, thereby holding the higher pressure trapped water until the next cycle. The air chamber indicated in 6 simply allows the action to occur reducing a hard hammering effect on the valves.

ESTHER, ADA, LUCY AND MARIAN IN HAY SLED
AT THE DEMAS PLACE

This was one of the Smith family's first visits to George and Esther at the Demas Place after their marriage. Picture was probably taken in the summer of 1917.

usually require a rope to be placed around the cow's neck, then extending down the cow's left side, outside of her left rear leg, and secured to her right rear leg just above her hock. If she attempted to kick the milker, who squatted on the right side near the udder, the rope jerked her neck and also bit into her left leg. A few days of this training usually made the cow quite aware of what was expected of her, and she stood quietly while milking took place.

Esther was a willing hand in helping George with many of these chores, including the milking of cows. She placed the milk in a cool place and let the cream rise to the top, whereby, she skimmed off the cream for use in desserts and other high calorie foods. Fresh milk was used for cooking and unused milk was allowed to curdle in a bucket, whereby, the cottage cheese was skimmed off for chicken feed and the whey was used for pig feed. Cream, that soured, was kept until enough was available for churning into butter. Butter was made from the cream by, using a simple glass jar, shaking the contents for an extended period of time. After the butter separated from the whey it was strained, then washed at least three times with cold water. Each washing involved the straining and vigorous "working" of the butter with a wooden paddle to squeeze out the excess whey. Salt was added to the finished product to achieve the proper flavor. In those days of meager income, even the salt was collected from seashore rocks that had depressions on top where evaporation had taken place. Many of these skills were learned from Lulu and Ada Harlan while she had stayed at the Harlan homestead.

All of the Harlans liked to have homemade bread on the table at all three meals of the day. Again, from those experiences during the previous 3 years, Esther became one of the best makers of raised homemade bread. She maintained a container of "starter yeast" for use in causing the bread to rise.

In addition to all of these activities Esther became quite a markswoman with the 410-gauge shotgun and would supplement their diet with brush rabbits bagged at the edges of the oat hayfield. George occasionally would bag a young buck from the "barley patch" and they would have fresh venison for a few days. Because there was no refrigeration, venison that was in excess was liberally sprinkled with black pepper and salt then hung on a wire to dry into jerky.

Esther had learned a lot about ranching in the Santa Lucias over these past six years and also learned to love the land, the scenery and all of the other things that the area could offer. She learned the names of nearly all of the trees, plants, grasses, animals, insects, reptiles, birds and even the rocks common to the area. She did not appreciate the numerous rattlesnakes that inhabited the area around the

Demas Place. Because the horses and cows and even the dogs would sometimes get bitten, George and Esther made sure that any one they saw did not live to possibly injure or kill them or one of the animals. In one summer season George killed more than forty rattlesnakes.

Esther did get quite homesick at the Demas Place because there was no telephone as there had been at the Harlan homestead. Mail service was only achieved when they would make the arduous trip to Esther's in-laws.

This trip did have its benefits, however. On the way to George's parents the trail crossed two major canyons, Big Creek and Vicente Creek. Each of these streams had good populations of rainbow trout, which Esther loved to catch and take home for a fish feast. She would typically catch a number of grasshoppers on the open ridges during the summer and enclose them live in a tobacco can for bait. A slender willow branch was used for a fish pole so only a short piece of line, a few hooks and some lead shot sinkers, stuck into her hat band, were all that was necessary to carry with her. It was not uncommon to catch 25 trout within a few holes of the trail crossing in an hour or less. The trout were typically 8 to 12 inches in length which made a nice feed for two people.

In 1919, an opportunity became available to move onto the Lopez homestead, very near the Harlan homestead. Aaron Wilber Harlan, George's older brother and the previous part owner, was called to serve in World War I. In his absence taxes and other loan payments fell delinquent and Monterey County declared the loans in default. The property was put up for public auction and George's father, Wilber, was the successful bidder. Wilber invited George and Esther to move onto the property since Aaron was still in the service.

All of the Lopez homestead was located in section seven of the 22nd township south and range 4 east of the Mt. Diablo meridian. One lot in section seven was later traded to Mr. and Mrs. Warren Gorrell in exchange for a similar plot of land in section eighteen, both adjacent to the seashore. This property included the projection of land known as Lopez Point, which is listed on contemporary maps of the region. There was a small split redwood cabin on this property which Manuel Lopez had started and Aaron Harlan had lived in for a short time. George later added a back porch, a front porch, a bathroom, two bedrooms, a pantry, a fireplace and some cupboards as time passed.

My father had only a few hand tools to work with in the early years. He was quite able at using natural materials in fabricating useful items. A highchair was made

ESTHER AND GEORGE HARLAN AT THE LOPEZ HOMESTEAD
CABIN WHERE THEY STARTED THEIR FAMILY
Circa 1919

This is the George and Esther Harlan home site where they raised their family of three sons. George added a front porch (visible on the left) and later added a bathroom and back porch in the area where they are seen in this photograph. He also added two bedrooms at the far end as the family grew.

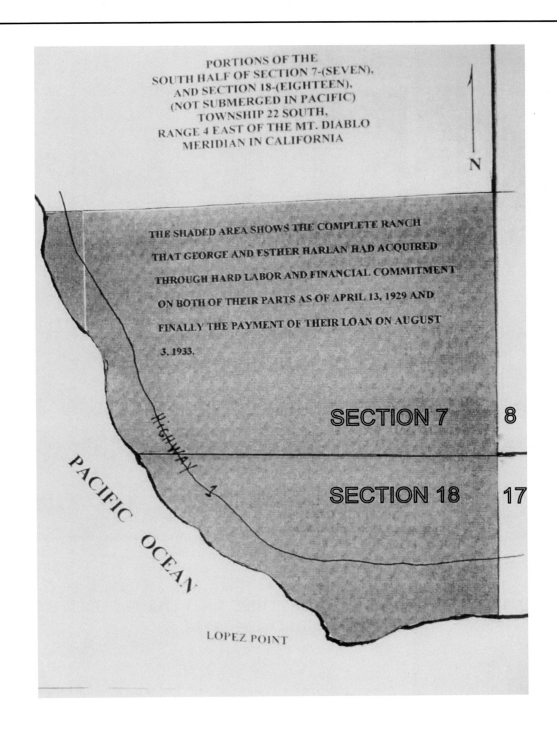

The shaded area shows the complete ranch that George and Esther Harlan had acquired through hard labor and financial commitment on both of their parts as of April 13, 1929 and finally the payment of their loan on August 3, 1933.

GRAPHICAL REPRESENTATION OF THE GEORGE AND ESTHER HARLAN RANCH
Parts of section 7 and 18 in township
22 south and range 4 east of the Mt. Diablo Meridian

AERIAL PHOTOGRAPH OF LOPEZ POINT AND THE HARLAN RANCH
AS IT APPEARED ON MAY 10, 2006

The red line indicates the approximate borders of the George and Esther Harlan ranch. Lopez Rock shows in the left foreground and Lopez Point is to the far lower right. An original photograph made for John Saar Properties has been modified by Stanley Harlan to show approximate property borders on that date.

Credits go to Realtor, Hillary Lipman and John Saar Properties who had contracted to have this photo taken of the ranch from the air when the ranch was put up for sale.

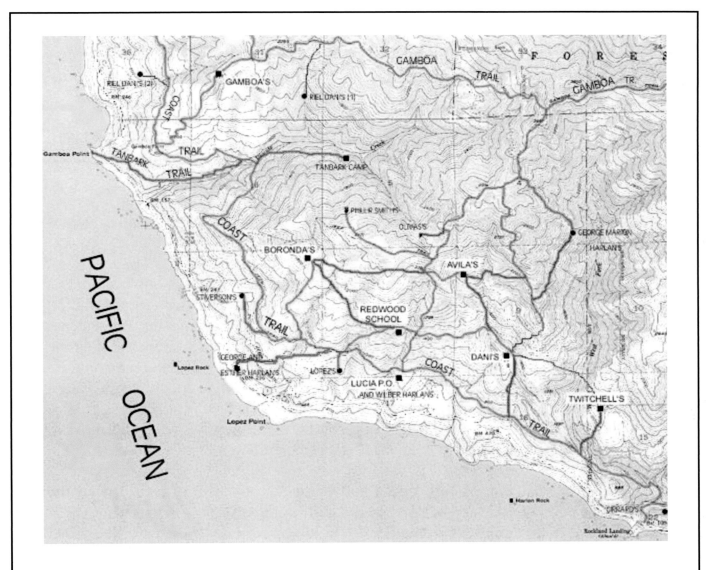

REFERENCES:

USGS 15 Minute Series, Lucia Quadrangle, 1921

Credits are made to "The Double Cone Quarterly"—Vol. 4 No. 1

Corrected and modified by Stanley Harlan

This map shows the relative locations of the homesteads in the Redwood School area and some of the trails connecting them. Students coming to school from the Girrards at lower right travelled nearly three miles as did the Riel Dani and Gamboa children from the other direction.

for Gene in 1922 from a few pieces of wood wired together. A full-size playpen was made from natural round limbs of redwood, willow, laurel and skunk berry (cascara) with holes bored with brace and bit to accommodate corner posts, rails, etc.

Aaron returned from the War with injuries and exposure to poison gas. Wilber J. Harlan again sold the property to Aaron upon his return, but Aaron found it hard to make payments on his new loan and chose to sell to George and Esther.

Life for George and Esther continued on here much as it had been at the Demas Place except they had much more to accomplish and also a debt to pay off.

About this time George acquired about a dozen angora goats from his uncle's homestead nearby. George Marion Harlan, a half-brother to my father's father, had died of a heart attack and left two young sons to manage the homestead. George M. Harlan had raised many goats on the property and my father took some of them when the boys sold out to George Gamboa. The goats were somewhat of a novelty. My father sheared them for a couple of years, then, he concentrated on his other tasks, letting the goats go "wild". They would sleep on the sheer face of the "Goat Rock" for protection against predators, then, they would spend most of the day getting into mischief in neighbor's gardens, etc.

There was a need to repair old fences and build new ones in order to make the ranch productive. Fences typically consisted of split redwood pickets about five and a half feet long and two by three inches in cross section. They were sharpened at one end with an axe by tapering each of its four surfaces about eight inches to a common point. The pickets were transported from the redwood canyon to the fence site by pack mule then driven into the ground with a maul. In rocky ground it was necessary to create a hole with a crow bar to accommodate the picket. Split redwood slats (about one inch thick, five to six feet long and four inches wide) were nailed onto the pickets about eight inches below the fence top. Heavier posts (five inches by seven inches by seven feet long) were used on each end of a gate opening or any other spot that needed reinforcement. These posts were also split from redwood logs in the canyons and transported to the fence site by mule. Holes were dug in the ground (typically one foot in diameter and thirty-two inches deep) for each post.

George split more lumber and roofing shakes from very straight grained redwood trees that grew on his father's timber claim in Vicente Creek. He hauled this material by horse and mule back nearly two miles to his new ranch, to make the

GEORGE ALWIN HARLAN WITH HIS ANGORA BILLY GOAT

He "inherited" about a dozen angora goats from his uncle, George Marion Harlan, when his uncle died. George M. Harlan's sons sold their father's homestead in Section 4 to George and Jake Gamboa and also dispensed their large goat herd before moving away from the coast.

George Alwin Harlan sheared his goats one or two years, then he let the herd go "wild". I remember being chased by the billy as a young boy.

STANLEY IN THE "HOMEMADE" PLAYPEN ON THE FRONT PORCH

1929

This picture shows how natural materials were utilized.

THE AXLE AND WHEELS FROM GEORGE AND ESTHER HARLAN'S
GO DEVIL MISSING THE WOODEN BODY AND TOUNGE

When George and Esther first started their ranch they only had home made sleds for hauling hay to the barn, rocks from the fields, pickets and posts to the fencing sites or any other heavy items that could not be carried on mule back. Their first investment in a wheeled vehicle was called a Go Devil. It proved to be a great improvement at the Lopez Point ranch because of a number of relatively flat fields. A single horse or mule hitched to it could haul hundreds of pounds at one time. Impressed with the Go Devil they soon invested in a four wheeled wagon drawn by a two-horse team. The wagon, pictured elsewhere in this tribute, became the main mode of hauling hay from the fields to the barn.

additions to the house and to build a barn, a granary, a pig shed and a chicken house.

The split redwood boards and the battens over each space did not make an air tight seal on the single walled structure of the house. Esther became inventive and gathered old magazines and newspapers from her neighbors and extended family over a period of time. She mixed flour and water to make a paste that she spread upon the walls and then attached layers of paper to seal up the open spaces. She then purchased rolls of wall paper which she attached the same way. The process worked surprisingly well and each room became quite cozy and decorative. All except the kitchen and pantry floors were treated in a similar manner and then she purchased sheets of linoleum as a finished surface for the floors. The kitchen and pantry floors and the two porches remained raw split lumber, and years of wear had made them
very uneven and hard to keep clean. Again she became inventive and, later on, when she had running water at the house, she used the garden hose and a nozzle to clean these floors on occasion.

Esther established garden plots around the house, and even though water had to be carried from a well near the house she became quite well known for her beautiful flowers and abundant varieties of vegetables. George somehow found time to make and to haul long redwood logs from the canyon to the house to form cribbing. These were fitted together on top of each other at intervals on the sloping hill to form terraces and consequently level garden beds between the house and the granary. Esther later received recognition for her garden by a national magazine. Quite a feat for a person located 50 miles from the nearest town accessible only by horseback or by boat.
All of section eighteen and parts of section seven bordered on the ocean. Esther, in addition to her love for trout fishing, also liked to go to the beach and gather abalone at low tide and fish for rock fish. Both of these provided many a meal for her and George in those early days.

A telephone extension was made to the party line that served the coastal families. About a mile of wire and a quite a number of redwood poles were required to reach the Wilber and Ada Harlan home. George, with the help of Marion, put this line in so Esther could call Lulu and other coastal people. She could also call her family in Campbell through the King City telephone exchange. Her number was 7-9-F-3-1, Wilber and Ada and Lulu 7-9-F-2-2, the Dani homestead 7-9-F-2-4, the Sipriano Avila ranch 7-9-F-1-5, etc. Esther and George could be reached by anyone on the party line by ringing three long period rings and one short period ring, or as we typically said--3 longs and a short. There were nearly 20 families on the party line (nearly 50 miles in length to King City) which had been installed in 1910 by Claude Harlan, George Marion Harlan's son, and the cooperative efforts of all who subscribed to the service. A fee was charged monthly to each member by Pacific Telephone Company for the privilege of connecting to the operator and people in King City (free of charge), and to make long distance calls for an extra fee. The King City operator was reached by ringing one "short" ring. All of the maintenance of the single wire line was the responsibility of the people who used it. After every winter storm it was necessary to walk the whole line to repair breaks, remove green growth from touching the wire, etc. Esther was a very social person and appreciated the telephone immensely.

Since Esther was within the Redwood School District boundary again, she was given the opportunity to fill any vacant time that became available at the school. She was called back for duty as a teacher there for a short period of time between September 20, 1920, and October 18, 1920. She was called again in 1922, from February 6th until April 28th according to official records at the Monterey County Schools office. There may be some discrepancy of these last dates, since Esther's first born son, Albert Eugene Harlan was born on April 7, 1921. I presume that another teacher substituted for Esther during part of this time period. Caring for a new baby simply added on another task for Esther, in addition to all the other responsibilities that she had. Things went well for the new Harlan family, and Gene, as he was called, prospered and grew rapidly to be a robust little boy. It was not long until he became a ready helper for his father in the many tasks that George took on.

It was during this time that George added on the last bedroom so the larger family could be accommodated. He used the same materials as before, but he made one change on the flooring. A sawmill at Mill Creek, about four miles south, had gone out of business and had left a stack of redwood 2 by 4s near the beach. George made arrangements to buy the lumber and his older brother, Aaron, agreed to tow it up the coast to Lopez Point behind his rowboat. On a calm day, the stack was bound together and George and Aaron put it afloat at Mill Creek, whereby Aaron got into his rowboat and started towing the mass of lumber north along the coast, using only the oars. George got back on his horse and rode the trail back to Lopez Point. Aaron was able to get there first, and he was waiting patiently for George when he arrived. The two of them beached the lumber and stacked it a safe distance up the bank in case of rough weather. Later on, George packed this lumber up the ocean bank (about 100 feet elevation) and then on to the house where he used it for flooring.

A TYPICAL RED AND BLACK ABALONE SHELL

Abalones were very numerous along the Big Sur coast shoreline during the years of my childhood and early adult life. They were harvested commercially by the Japanese divers from diving boats (we called them "trailers") before World War II. The abalone launches came from their home port of Monterey pulling their diving boats behind them at some distance. They would anchor the launches in the protection of Lopez Point Bay, then, they made daytime diving excursions within a few miles of the anchorage. There were more than 12 launches in the group and after 3 days of diving they would load up their catch from floating wooden crates and head to Monterey in their launch, leaving the diving boats behind in the anchorage. Typically, the launches were loaded with hundreds of dozens of red abalones on each trip.

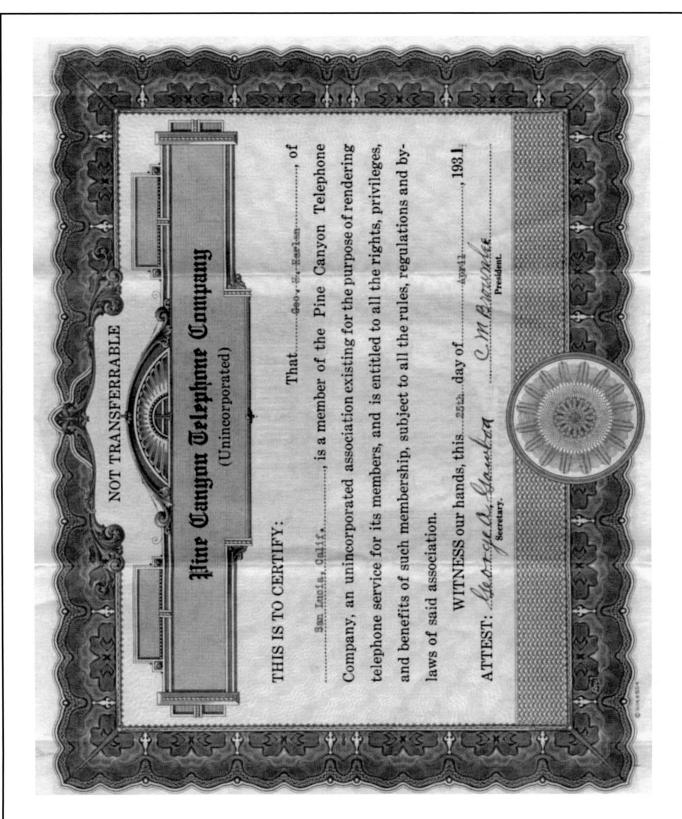

NOT TRANSFERRABLE

Pine Canyon Telephone Company
(Unincorporated)

THIS IS TO CERTIFY:

That Geo. H. Harlan , of San Lucia, Calif. , is a member of the Pine Canyon Telephone Company, an unincorporated association existing for the purpose of rendering telephone service for its members, and is entitled to all the rights, privileges, and benefits of such membership, subject to all the rules, regulations and by-laws of said association.

WITNESS our hands, this 25th. day of April , 1931.

ATTEST: George A. Gaeths
Secretary.

C. M. Brownlee
President.

TELEPHONE MEMBER CERTIFICATE FOR THE HARLANS

Through all of this Esther prospered, and on May 11, 1925, she gave birth to her second son, Donald Alwin Harlan, and two and a half years later, a third son, Stanley Vernon Harlan, on November 11, 1927.

Lack of running water at the house was always a problem and about 1928, my mother and father purchased enough cement to make a water tank at a spring of water above the house. The water tank was approximately a 6-foot cube on the inner dimensions which held about 1500 gallons of water. The walls and bottom of the tank were about 6 inches in thickness. The excavation was all done by hand for the foundation of the tank. The cement was purchased in 90-pound sacks and all the sand and gravel was hauled in "gunny sacks" from the beach by mule back. The materials for the concrete structure weighed approximately 10,000 pounds. It was a major challenge to haul this much aggregate to the site. The concrete was all mixed by hand with a garden hoe. George made a galvanized sheet metal tub about a foot deep and 3 feet wide and 4 feet long with wooden sides for the hand mixing operation. The seams were riveted and soldered to make the tub water proof. Sufficient galvanized water pipe was purchased to reach from the tank to the house (about 600 feet). Considering the crude methods by which these kinds of projects were accomplished, bringing a supply of fresh water to the house under gravity pressure was a major undertaking, as were most of the other achievements they completed. My mother found this addition to be a great improvement to her standard of living. She no longer had to dip water out of the well with a bucket. The extra washing of baby clothes was quite an extra burden on her, however.

In these days she typically put an oblong copper tub (about 20 gallons, with a tin coating inside) on the wood stove about two thirds full of water. In this water she would submerge the white clothing to be washed and add about a bar of finely cut Fels Naptha bar soap. When the water came to a boil she would stir the contents with a round wooden stick (part of an old broom handle) for an extended period of time. When she was satisfied that the clothes were clean, she would lift the hot clothes out of the tub with the stirring stick and place them into a large pan nearby. She would then throw in all of the dirty overalls and heavy shirts into the hot tub of water and add some more soap. The pan of washed clothes she would take to the back porch where she had double wash trays. Hot water produced by a water coil in the wood stove, and a storage tank behind the stove, was piped to the wash trays for rinsing all of the clothes by hand. She later got a hand operated "wringer" that clamped onto the vertical wall of the wash trays.

A PROUD FATHER, GEORGE, HOLDING HIS SON, GENE, ON THE PORCH ROOF THAT GEORGE IS WORKING ON.

GENE SITTING IN "HOMEMADE" HIGH CHAIR IN BACK YARD

Circa 1923

With new members in the family my grandmother, Lucy Farrell Smith, and my mother's two younger and unmarried sisters, Maude Marian and Ada Eleanor, came regularly to the ranch during the summer months for an extended visit with us. It was necessary for them to take the mountain trail from the "Cave" to the coast by horseback as my mother had done in 1913. My aunts were both teachers, and they looked forward to visiting the ranch each year during the summer vacation period.

Leonard, who operated a garage in Campbell, would take a couple of weeks off in August each year and also come to the ranch for a visit with the rest of the family. He liked to hunt, and he would usually bring his wife, Ruth, and two children, Bayard and Stephanie. He also would bring a close friend, either George Whipple or Harry Hathaway, with him. Everyone seemed to bring us "something". Mr. Whipple, who owned an orchard, would bring fresh fruit in large quantities for eating fresh and for canning. The aunts would bring us toys and fireworks for the Fourth of July. We all looked forward to these times, even though there was more work to be done but also more hands to do it. My mother would set up folding camp cots on the front porch for sleeping and there was another bed in the granary that was sometimes used.

Through the urging of my mother's brother, Leonard (who was mechanically minded), my father decided to buy a wind electrical generating machine (which we called a windmill) and 56 large glass electric cells (weighing about 60 lbs. each) to form a battery system delivering 112 volts of direct current. It has been said that this particular system was the first purchased west of the Mississippi.

The cells were arranged in rows on redwood shelving at different levels in part of our granary. The cells were connected in series with lead strips approximately 10 inches long, ¼ inch thick and 1 inch wide with a single lead coated brass bolt at each end solidly connecting them to the corresponding cell post.

The generator was capable of producing 1,000 watts of power in a moderate wind. Its ratings were as follows: Model BE 11--serial number 77534--3 to 1 gear ratio--time continuous--55-degree centigrade rise--130 volts direct current--7.7 ampere output--differential compound windings--700 to 2500 rpm.

A site had been selected on top of a ridge about 150 yards from the house for locating the tower for mounting the electrical generating machine. This location was in a very exposed location for both, the west winds, which blew predominately, and the south winds, which preceded most stormy weather.

DONALD, GENE AND STANLEY ABOVE THE OLD HARLAN
HOME IN 1929

George and Esther had forged a family of three boys on the Lopez Point Ranch. Times were difficult in the Great Depression years and into the 1930's as well. My mother always saw to it that the three of us were always dressed warmly as the woolen leggings indicate. She found it a challenge to keep us clean. Our playgrounds were the dirt banks around the house.

Heavy and ponderous equipment like this was delivered by coastal steamer out of San Francisco, to an off-shore anchorage near our ranch. The freight was then transferred to a row boat for landing on our beach. There was an unassembled galvanized steel tower, a large fan-like tail piece, the gearbox and generator, and heavy insulated copper wire to connect the wind generator to the storage batteries in the granary near the house. Also among the items delivered was a heavy slate electric controller panel with a volt meter, an amp meter, and a cut-out coil that disconnected the circuit to the batteries if the voltage from the generator fell below 112 volts. There were also insulators, a propeller (airplane like, and about 10 feet long), and lots of nuts and bolts. Amazingly, nothing was missing, broken or lost in transit. Landing these materials on the beach or packing them nearly a mile to the assembly site by mules was also successful. The battery cells alone took 28 round trips by placing a single cell on each side of the mule in a pack saddle.

It was also necessary to carry cement, sand and gravel from the beach to the construction site to make a secure foundation for each of the four legs. A large hole was made in the ground for each "leg" position. Then each hole was filled to grade with hand mixed concrete. Within each of these four concrete foundations the leg angle irons for the tower were embedded.

My dad was one to always make things very strong and "proper", and these foundations and the tower are still intact today. There were two power poles supporting the wires from the windmill generator to the granary. Babe, our trustworthy horse, pulled those redwood poles for about a mile from one of our redwood canyons over a narrow mountain trail to the intended pole sites. My father always made post holes for fencing 32 inches deep and power pole holes five feet deep. When he no longer could reach the bottom of the hole with his arms to remove the loose dirt and rock he would call one of us over to help him. He would hold us by the ankles and suspend our body upside down in the hole. By alternately lifting one of us up and down we were able to scoop out the loose material with a discarded abalone shell.

The site was well selected and, after everything was assembled, our family was one of the first to enjoy 112-volt direct current electrical power. The winds did not always blow when the need was greatest, so we had to use the electricity with cautious restraint. My mother purchased a washing machine with a direct current motor and she would time the washings to coincide with the windy days.

The windmill required constant attention by all concerned. A strong wind, sometimes reaching 80 to 90 miles an hour, would cause the windmill to turn too fast, thereby making the generator and tail assembly swing wildly from side to side and result in a shuddering vibration. It would also charge at a higher rate than it was designed for, causing an overcharge of the batteries. These circumstances would require that we feather the tail so the propeller did not face into the wind. This procedure required us to crank a handle at the base of the tower, which caused the tail axis to rest at a 90-degree angle in relationship to the propeller. Performing this operation became known as "turning the windmill off". Reversing the procedure was termed "turning the windmill on". My brothers and I climbed the hill from the house to the windmill many hundreds of times to perform one of these operations or the other. I can still hear my mother call, "Stanley, go up and turn the windmill on", or, "Donald, go up and turn the windmill off."

My father not only ran his ranching operation but also spent much time clearing brush from usable plots of land. He would grub the smaller brush by hand with a mattock then cut the larger growth with an axe and pile it for burning. After burning it was necessary to grub out the stumps with the mattock as well. He would sow these selected areas with barley and, to cover the seed with soil, he would hitch a single horse to a spring tooth (a rectangular frame of metal with adjustable spring steel teeth attached) and drag it over the area.

He raised oat hay in selected areas on the ranch where fences or natural barriers would prevent livestock intrusion. On the steeper slopes, he cut the oat hay with a scythe, and after curing, he hauled it to the barn on a sled drawn by one or two horses. On the flatter sections of land, he tilled the soil with a side hill plow, drawn by a team of two horses, broadcast the seed grain by hand, and then harrowed the area to break the clods and to cover the seed. Upon maturity, the hay was cut with a two-horse team drawn mowing machine (McCormick Deering Big-6 mower), which cut about a five-foot swath at a time. After a few days of drying in the field the hay was raked with a horse drawn rake and left in windrows for further drying. The windrows were then converted into "shocks" of hay by hand with a pitchfork, where they remained for another two weeks for additional curing. The shocks were then loaded onto a sled (or later a wagon) and hauled to the barn for storage for winter use.

All of these activities would lead one to believe that there would not have been time in the day to accomplish more. However, in 1922, George successfully bid on, and won, the responsibility of carrying the mail, once weekly, from Jolon to the coastal families along the way, and finally to the Lucia Post Office, which was located in the Wilber Harlan home. On the return to Jolon, he was responsible to carry out any letters or other mail from the Lucia Post Office and to also pick up

THE WINDMILL TOWER WHICH STILL STANDS
(IN 2007) ON ORIGINAL FOOTINGS

The propeller and generator were removed from the tower in 1947 since my mother and father had moved to the Nesbitt ranch temporarily and did not want to leave the windmill un-attended.

ADAM WOOD, MY GRANDSON, HOLDING THE ORIGINAL PROPELLER
FROM OUR WINDMILL

*It is 10 feet in length, made of wood with sheet metal on the leading edges and with
a steel hub which mounted onto the gearbox.*

THE WINDMILL GENERATOR WITH ATTACHED GEAR BOX

The base of the generator was bolted to a freely rotating saddle at the top of the tower so the attached tail assembly would turn the front of the generator and propeller into the wind direction. The propeller was attached to the tapered shaft at the front of the gear box. The gears turned in a bath of gear oil and the oil level was maintained by oil seals on the input shaft from the propeller and the shaft leading to the generator at the rear of the gear box.

The two wires carrying the direct current generator output exited the generator at the center of its base in the saddle and fed collector rings and electrical brushes at the top of the tower. From there the wires led to insulators on a nearby pole and then to another pole before entering the battery bank in our granary about 100 yards distant.

A VIEW OF THE GEARS WITHIN THE WINDMILL GEAR BOX

After approximately 30 years of service, and then many more years of exposure, this is the present condition of the gears within the gearbox of the windmill. They show very little wear and it speaks very highly of the manufacturer and the design of the equipment.

Brief, but conservative, calculations would indicate the larger gear, which held 48 teeth, has turned at least 5 trillion times in its productive life and the generator gear, with 18 teeth, has managed 3 times as many turns.

The propeller caused the generator to turn three times for every single revolution it made.

other outgoing mail along the way. He purchased a Graham-Paige, open side panel delivery truck, which he used to bring the mail from Jolon to the White ranch in the Nacimiento River valley. There, he transferred the mail to his pack animals (usually a horse, Bunch, and two mules, Little Jack and Big Jack, and sometimes more mules, which he kept available at the White Ranch) and traversed the Santa Lucia Mountain Range to his destination on the coast.

These trips were sometimes routine and other times very far from it. There was always extra mail during the holiday season which required more mules in the pack train. Local people also ordered large objects, such as harrows, spring tooths, pipe, washtubs and other similar objects through the catalog mail order stores, as well, which he had to figure out some way to deliver.

On one occasion, my father had a harrow to deliver and he loaded it onto one the "extra mules" who was not thoroughly broken for packing. He was very careful in the loading process, making sure that the mule was kept calm. When he was tying the final hitch, the mule started to buck with that "unfamiliar" package on his back, and my father could only try to get out of the way. The mule went through all sorts of contortions and finally the harrow shifted to where one of the metal teeth came in contact with his body. This mule, typical of the breed, was noted for his sharp mental abilities, and he literally "froze his motions" until my father came over to repack the harrow. From that day on, this mule never did offer to buck with a load again.

Typically, my father would follow the Nacimiento River bottom from the White Ranch to the McKern Trail where he reached the mountain top near the head of Mill Creek. This route required crossing the Nacimiento River many times. On some occasions, during the winter, the weather would be stormy and raining. The streams would be swollen to almost flood stage, and the Nacimiento River could only be crossed by swimming the horse and mules. In this weather he often had to take a longer route, further south on the Los Burros trail to the top of the mountain to prevent crossing the river more than once. Keeping the mail dry meant extra steps had to be taken in the packing process. This caused him to be late in starting for the coast and he frequently ended up in the dark along the trail. The animals, with somewhat better night vision, could navigate the familiar trail even in the dark. On one windy night, however, trees had fallen ahead of him and also behind him, blocking the trail completely. By chance, he was not too far from one of the homestead houses, and he called out at the top of his lungs for help (my father was noted for his ability to call out in a thunderous voice when necessary). He was able to get a response as he saw a lit kerosene lantern moving up the hill through

SIDEHILL PLOW THAT WAS USED BY GEORGE HARLAN
ON HIS RANCH AT LOPEZ POINT

Drawn by a two-horse team this implement allowed the plowing of sloping land so hay or other crops could be planted. The plow is set to turn a furrow to the right as it is seen here. At the end of the field the plow share and mold board could be rotated to face on the opposite side, thereby, allowing the team and plow to turn around and still turn the furrow toward the plowed land.

ANOTHER VIEW OF THE SIDEHILL PLOW SHOWING THE LAND
SLIDE AND MECHANISM FOR ROTATING THE PLOW SHARE
AND MOLD BOARD TO THE OPOSITE SIDE

This implement was sometimes used with a single mule or horse to build trails on the ranch as well. Another application was to loosen soil that was to be excavated for a structure such as a barn. My father would usually plow my mother's vegetable garden in the spring for her plantings, and he also plowed a remote plot of ground for planting a years supply of potatoes and corn.

WILBER AND AARON HARLAN HAULING HAY FROM THE SIDEHILL
FIELD TO THE BARN ON A SLED

In the early days this chore was labor intensive and on the steep slopes it was the "only" way. Note the horse and mule "taking on fuel", a benefit of working with that sweet fresh hay.

the wind and the rain. With the welcome help of this neighbor they were able to clear the trail and my dad was able to continue on his way.

On another trip, during the summer, my father heard the familiar buzzing of a rattlesnake. The horse and mules became quite erotic and charged down the trail. The snake continued to rattle, however, even after they had gone a considerable distance. The sound seemed to be close at hand, and as my father turned around in the saddle he saw the large rattler slide off of the rear apron of the saddle, hitting the ground with a "plop". The snake had evidently struck out at the horse, or my dad, from a high bank next to the trail and his momentum carried him onto the horse's withers, where he rode a short distance, rattling all the while.

On many trips the pack train was followed by a mountain lion. I have heard that mountain lions do not make much of a sound, but my father said he knew this was a mountain lion because of the way the animals reacted. It made a shrill whistling sound repeatedly as the lion would follow the pack animals. On these occasions my father would check the trail for tracks on his next trip out, and sure enough, a large lion's track would appear on top of his mule tracks from the previous trip through these areas where he heard the lion, and where the pack animals were very uneasy. On one trip, the lion followed him all of the way to the ranch, and the next morning my father's dog, Tag, treed the lion within a half mile of the house.

While George was off on the mail route (at least two full days every week), Esther took care of all of the responsibilities on the ranch. She took care of Gene, fed the pigs, fed the chickens, milked the cows and a myriad other planned, and unplanned, chores. Fences had to be mended where pigs rooted out pickets, firewood had to be cut with a buck saw for the stove, calves had to be fed and shut in the manger of the barn each night. Our dogs were trained to tree animals that may harm the livestock so, frequently, in the middle of the night, Esther would have to get up and go to where the dogs had treed an animal and shoot it with the 410 shotgun. As Gene got bigger he helped on many of the lighter chores, such as feeding the chickens, gathering the eggs from the chickens, closing the chickens in at night, feeding the dogs, etc.

On one occasion my mother had to collect a sow with her newborn piglets nearly a mile away from the pen. If she were to leave the sow and her piglets out in the wild, the coyotes would have finished the little ones off. She had never done anything like this before, and the sow was threatening her presence in the area. She sent Gene home to get his little red wagon. Upon Gene's return with the wagon, which he had pulled through two major pastures and along a narrow trail to

AN EXAMPLE OF A COMMON SPIKE TOOTHED HARROW

This implement was used to break up clods formed in the plowing process. It also was effective in covering the broadcast grain seed so the seed would sprout in the damp soil. A single horse could pull one of these through the field to accomplish the above results. It was not uncommon to connect two or three harrows side by side to accomplish the task at hand much quicker with a two-horse team.

Implements like this were sometimes ordered by mail through the Montgomery Ward catalog and were delivered to the coastal settlers by the mail carrier on mule back. They were a challenging load for a mule, not too heavy, but very cumbersome. Larger implements had to be disassembled for shipping by these methods.

A TYPICAL SPRING TOOTHED HARROW USED BY THE PIONEER
FAMILIES ALONG THE BIG SUR COAST

This implement, drawn by a single horse or mule, was used to loosen the soil and mix the ashes on freshly burned ground to cover the freshly sown barley seed. Each tooth was, in effect, a large spring that would not easily get hung up on a protruding root, rock or stump. A trained horse and teamster could maneuver the spring toothed harrow across a fairly steep side hill with amazing results.

The selective burning of brushy sidehills followed by growing a stand of barley was a very successful technique of all the early pioneers in this area. It taught skills of farming to the children of the pioneer families, and it also provided them with experience of producing a cash crop to get them started in life.

GEORGE HARLAN ON HIS MAIL ROUTE

This picture represents how the mail was delivered from the inner valley at Jolon to the Lucia Post Office on the coast near Lopez Point. George typically rode a lead horse and led two or more mules with pack saddles and their loads of mail order cargo, packages and mail over the many miles of narrow, mountain trails.

get back to the site of the sow's nest. My mother alternately gave the sow some corn and slyly picked up one pig at a time and put each one in a sack until all were accounted for. The sow made a number of threats but stopped short of biting her. Marian Smith, Esther's sister, and Gene then pulled the wagon back home, and Esther carried one of the sacks--pigs a squealing and the sow following closely behind. My Aunt Marian had written up this experience and I would like to include it here:

A SATURDAY SURPRISE

This is an incident that took place on the Harlan ranch long ago. Memory of the time is still sharp, and a feeling of amusement creeps into the telling.

George was on the weekly mail route so he was not home. He had left with his pack train early on Friday, and wouldn't be home until late Saturday--a long and responsible trip.

George had turned the penned up pigs loose to eat the large tan oak acorns, which had begun to fall. He knew that, before long, some piglets were due, but, of course, he wasn't sure just when. He hoped they would arrive the first of the week when he would be home.

We learned that the sow had her family when Saturday morning arrived. They were a distance from the house near the Ranchito Creek.

Essie, of course, always concerned about all living creatures, large of small, had visions of the tiny porkers being snatched away by coyotes, endangering the sow and losing the piglets.

Essie decided that we should go and bring them home for safety in the pig pen. Coyotes are fond of pork and work in pairs. One engages the attention of the sow and the other steals a pig. Then one coyote gets the piglet away to a safe distance before both feast.

Our mother, Lucy Smith, couldn't manage to go at the pace necessary to reach the place where the sow was, so she and Don stayed home to care for things there. Don was a little fellow and would have liked to go to, but was told hurriedly that he was to take care of Grandma.

Away we went, Gene, Essie, Ada and I, carrying sacks to transport the babies home. Ada and I had never had anything to do with pigs on the loose. Essie was a worried adult, and Gene was looking forward to an exciting time.

We found the sow and eight little ones--"Mama" grunting proudly. All was well until we tried to get near the new family. Gene caught one and put it into the sack--squealing to high heaven. "Mama" dashed at Gene, who put the sack down--quickly! The sow smelled the sack and grunted soothingly to her offspring. Essie, in the meantime, had stuffed a baby into the other sack. More squeals and a dash by the sow snuffing and objecting.

Essie was worried for everything! Someone might be hurt by the sow! The tiny pink-footed and pink-nosed little bits of nature might be injured! The hogs in the area might be attracted by the noise!

To make a long story shorter, Gene ran home for his little red wagon. While he was gone we managed to get the piglets into the sacks.

It was no easy job to get the noisy, wiggly sack into the little red wagon, but we managed--dog barking, sow protesting and adults apprehensive.

Essie carried the second wiggling sack. Each time a piggy squealed Essie put the sack down for the sow to smell and give comforting "speech" to the captives. They replied with perfect understanding.

Those in the little red wagon were steadied by Ada or me, and kernels of corn were tossed to the sow to get her attention away from the sack.

Perhaps she realized we were not such monsters after all, as we moved toward the barn by stops and starts--each person doing what he could to help--carry the sack, push or pull the wagon, steady the load, or keep the sow's mind on corn tossed her way.

Like all mothers, sows can be very possessive of their charges, and can be extremely dangerous. Anyone who has heard a hog chomp its teeth knows the danger. They can move very fast as well.

Along with all the activity and danger there was a lot of laughter, exclamations, warnings and happy chatter.

The pen, prepared ahead of time with toothsome provisions and new straw and water, was finally reached. With quick movements, and little ceremony, the piggies were put into the pen.

"Mama", after examining her family, went to the feed trough, ate, and then lay down, grunting contentedly as the little ones suckled.

During the next days there were many many trips to admire, fondle and be enchanted by the little pigs who had learned to squeeze out of the pen. They loved being handled and "Mama" seemed to be proud of both family and special treats that came her way.

Soon the creatures were little butterballs, still with pink noses and tiny little feet. Really adorable! Anyone who has not held a little porker has really missed something.

M. Marian Smith—1990

It was about this time that my father fenced in a large rectangular garden area, on nearly flat ground, for my mother, near a water well, in one of the fields below the house. It was as though my mother did not have enough to do. One of my first memories was to be trundled down through the field in a large wheeled baby buggy (perambulator) to the garden area. My brother, Donald was old enough to walk along with my mother, while Gene was off to school or with my father helping with his chores. At the garden site, my mother vigorously spaded the ground, raked it smooth and planted seeds of an extensive variety of vegetables. She lifted buckets of water from the well to nourish those plants already started. After each session at the "garden", my mother would push me and a selection of vegetables back up to the house in the baby carriage.

At one side of the garden, my father had totally enclosed an area, including the top, about 10 feet wide and 30 feet long, with one-inch mesh wire poultry netting, for the exclusive purpose of raising strawberries. As a result of my father's and mother's hard work we enjoyed strawberries in all forms from this enclosure for a number of years. California Valley Quail used their ingenuity to "dust" themselves adjacent to the edge of the base board, which held the bottom edge of the wire, thereby creating a depression of the soil, by which they could gain access to the enclosure and all those ripe strawberries. On many occasions it became our responsibility to "catch" the quail and turn them loose outside. They were perfectly happy to stay in the enclosed area, taking their pick of the strawberries and bugs and enjoying their safety from Cooper's Hawks and other predators.

My mother was kept very busy taking care of three young sons along with all of the other activities. She could not take on more teaching until the school year of 1928-1929. She taught all of that year and every year thereafter until June of 1942. The school, due to lack of attendance, was suspended for two years from the fall of 1922 to the spring of 1924. Two years later, it was threatened with closure for the same reason but with the importation of a few students and combining it with an adjacent school district, it was kept open. Because it became part of the San Antonio School District the name changed to Redwood Branch School.

There were other major changes at the school as well. Many of the homesteaders sold out to larger land interests in the 1920s and 1930s, and in 1933 the coastal highway was being constructed in the area. These changes caused the school to serve more families at the lower elevation near the highway construction area. The old Redwood School site was abandoned for temporary locations in a corrugated metal building on the George Harlan Ranch, then to a temporary tent, and finally to

MARIAN SMITH AND DONALD HARLAN AT ESTHER HARLAN'S
VEGETABLE GARDEN BY THE OLD WELL
JUNE 1937

This garden was in the field about ¼ mile below and somewhat south of our old house. My mother grew all kinds of vegetables here for a number of years. There was a well in the corner behind Donald's image. Water was lifted from the well with a rope and bucket at first. Later, my father installed a hand pump and a containment trough. Water could be siphoned from the trough to all parts of the garden with garden hoses. Donald and I usually manned the pump while my mother selectively watered her garden.

the George and Esther Harlan home site, until another school building could be constructed near the highway.

My father also took on extra work during the late 1920's to augment his cash income. In addition to all of his other responsibilities he worked part time for the three investors who had purchased the Big Creek property. They were Warren Gorrell, John Marble and Frank O. Horton[2]. The investors had a plan to make the Big Creek area into a novel dude ranch with fishing, hunting, hot spring bathing and outdoor relaxation for the moneyed class. Their plan included a landing at the beach at the mouth of Big Creek and a wagon road to the Hot Springs in the north fork of Big Creek. Also included was a captive trout farm near the creek bottom about 300 yards upstream from the mouth of Big Creek.

There were other people employed by the investment group on these projects from time to time. Marion David Harlan, my father's younger brother, was employed to measure the water flow in the streams on the property during this period of time. Tony Fontes was hired to help out on many of the activities particularly related to the training of horses used on the ranch. Henry Porter was employed to cut and haul wood for the ranch and he also was hired to use his boat to go to Monterey for supplies used at the fledgling ranch. Henry Trotter (Sam Trotter's son), Bill Foster, Kene Crivelli, Al Holland, Martin Anderson and Earl Rice also worked on various projects on the ranch.

Sam Trotter was employed to build two bridges of natural logs and timbers at a crossing just above the forks of the creek and another across the north fork of Big Creek a little farther upstream. Sam Trotter was a legend of the area for many years. His understanding of mechanical devices combined with his super human physical strength culminated in his many outstanding accomplishments in the south coast area. He completed these two bridges while my father was working on other parts of the project.

---

[2] HORTON, Frank Ogilvie, a Representative from Wyoming; born in Muscatine, Muscatine County, Iowa, October 18, 1882; attended the public schools; was graduated from Morgan Park (Ill.) Military Academy in 1899 and from the University of Chicago in 1903; during the Spanish-American War served as a private in Company C, Fiftieth Iowa Regiment, in 1898; moved to Saddlestring, Wyo., in 1905 and engaged in livestock raising; member of the State house of representatives 1921-1923; served in the State senate 1923-1931, being president in 1931; delegate to the Republican National Conventions in 1928 and 1936; Republican National committeeman 1937-1948; elected as a Republican to the Seventy-sixth Congress (January 3, 1939-January 3, 1941); unsuccessful candidate for reelection in 1940 to the Seventy-seventh Congress; resumed his former pursuits in Saddlestring, Wyo.; died in Sheridan, Wyo., August 17, 1948; interment in Willowgrove Cemetery, Buffalo, Wyo.

George, my father, worked (for $4 a day or $5 a day with mule) on a number of projects that were going on at Big Creek. He created the bed for the 3 inch galvanized steel piping that was to feed water to the concrete fish pond. The intake was a fair distance upstream from the pond and it required much hand drilling and blasting of rock to create a graded bed for the pipe to rest in.

He built the road up the bottom of the creek to a point a few yards upstream from the two major forks. He did this by hand, using a star drill and a hammer to drill holes, then, using dynamite for blasting rock formations, and finally using a sledge hammer, pick and shovel and crowbar to reduce pieces to a manageable size. He loaded the rubble onto a wooden sled and his mules then pulled the sled to an unloading area to create fills in the low areas. He continued this cut and fill method on the southeast side of the stream at slightly above the high-water mark. Much of this roadway is still in use today though it has been widened somewhat and stone wall cribbing has been added in a place or two by the Moore work crews and by those of more recent ownership.

My father sometimes worked in the north fork of Big Creek, near the Hot Springs, for the investment group. Here, he split fence posts from fallen redwood trees. He used an eight-foot timber saw to cut log sections 7 feet long by hand. A mall and wedges were used to split the 7-foot logs into 5 by 7-inch fence posts.

Gene remembers being asked by his mother to take his father's horse, Bunch, over to his dad, near the hot spring, along with lunch and other food for his stay away from home. The distance was 5 or 6 miles from the ranch and the narrow Coast Trail wound through many dark canyons along the way. Gene relates the fact that his hair was standing on end most of the way and that is why his hair has remained standing to a noticeable extent ever since. Gene was only 9 or 10 years old at the time.

I can relate to his feelings a few years later when I was asked to deliver a message to Gene at our white guest house, where Gene slept, about a half mile distant from our house. It was late in the evening in January 1940. The south wind was blowing hard and there was a threat of imminent rain. I was alone on the trail when I came face to face with a large bobcat coming down the steep trail toward me. He was as frightened as me but could not get traction to run away on the gravelly surface of the trail. He actually jumped on my thigh to make his turn and I could only utter a "soundless" scream. He had not realized I was there because of

THE GEORGE AND ESTHER HARLAN FAMILY IN THE LATE 1930'S

Left to right—Gene, (Browny), Stanley, Esther, Donald & George

This picture was taken by Lester Liebenberg who was hired by my father to do some bulldozer work on a new road to our white guest house. This was still in the days when we were doing all of the ranch work by hand or with the aid of horses or mules. The location of the picture is just below the front porch of our old house in section 7.

GUEST HOUSE AT THE MARBLE PLACE
Circa 1931

This was a modern type building constructed by a professional carpenter with some help from my father, George Harlan. My father hauled all the materials for this house with his mules up the steep "zig zag" trail which is still maintained in a similar form by the University of California today. The materials had been shipped by boat from either Monterey or San Francisco to the beach at the mouth of Big Creek. He did this while working for the investment group, Frank O. Horton, John Marble and Warren Gorrell.

Due to the Great Depression, and the collapse of the economy and the investment group, this house was never used until many years later by the University of California for a study center. It burned to the ground in the Rat Creek Fire of 1985. It has since been replaced by another study center.

the very strong wind and the loud noises of the swaying branches of nearby brush and tree limbs.

My father also built a trail from the terminus of the road through the timbered side hill to the Marble Place (now called Whale Point by the University). He also hauled all of the lumber and other modern building materials by pack mule, from the beach at the mouth of Big Creek, up the zig zag trail to the Marble Place as well. He worked with a professional carpenter in the construction of the Guest House that was built there by the investment group. Another project that my father worked on was development of the natural water spring just below the guest house. He created a reservoir at the spring location by building a small concrete dam. Then he installed a gasoline engine and water pump of the day and the water was forced up the hill through a steel pipe to a tank situated above the old homestead house. This system, with more modern modifications, served the successive owners of the property until very recently in 2009.

The Great Depression of 1929 brought all of these developments to a standstill. My father received a letter dated the 10th of October, 1930 from Frank O. Horton, the main source of financing and who also had a ranch near Buffalo, Wyoming, stating that all work at the ranch was to cease until further notice. Much more was done in 1931 and even in 1932, but my father, one of the last to work for the investment trio, put in his last half day on November 24, 1932. My father had to look elsewhere for cash income.

There was still a balance to be paid for the ranch and it became necessary for George and Esther to take out a loan to cover those commitments. The Great Depression was not yet in recovery and banks were reluctant to make a loan without collateral. On January 2, 1932 they did acquire a chattel mortgage by putting up everything they owned for security. This was an unfamiliar step for both of my parents and we were too young to recognize the severity of the situation. It was only through their willingness to work long hours with little financial reward that brought them through this crisis. A likeness of the Chattel Mortgage follows:

"CHATTEL MORTGAGE

(INDIVIDUAL MORTGAGOR AND CORPORATION MORTGAGKE)

THIS MORTGAGE, made and entered into this 2nd. day of January, 1932, by and between Geo. A. Harlan and M. Esther Harlan, husband and wife of

the County of Monterey, State of California, the parties of the first
part, hereinafter called the Mortgagors, and MONTEREY COUNTY TRUST &
SAVINGS BANK a corporation organized and existing under and by virtue
of the laws of the States of California the party of the second part, hereinafter called the
Mortgagee,

WITNESSETH:

That said Mortgagors mortgage to the said mortgagee all the following described personal property, together with the increase thereof, if
any, situated in the County of Monterey, State of California, and described
as follows, to wit:

26 head stock cows branded *GH* on right hip,

12 head 2 year old heifers branded *GH* on right hip

12 head 2 year old steers branded *GH* on right hip

11 head yearling heifers branded *GH* on right hip

9 head yearling steers branded *GH* on right hip

12 head calves branded *GH* on right hip

2 head stock cows branded *GH* on right hip

10 head mixed calves branded *GH* on right hip.

All of the above live stock now being situate on the lands of the
mortgagors, located about one mile NW of Lucia post office on the Coast,
about 50 miles SW of King City, in the County of Monterey, State of California.

Together with the increase thereof, accretions or additions to all
of the above live stock, and all animals becoming a part of said herd as
replacements of animals dying, lost, sold, or exchanged.
as security for the payment to the said mortgagee of the sum of Six Hundred
& No/100 dollars ($600.00), in Gold Coin of the United States of America,
with interest thereon according to the terms of a certain promissory note
of even date herewith, executed by and delivered by the said Mortgagors
to the said Mortgagee, and which said note s in the words and figures
as follows, to wit:

$600.00   King City, Calif.   Jan 2, 1932.

On Demand after date, for value received I, we, or either of us
promise to pay to MONTEREY COUNTY TRUST AND SAVINGS BANK a corporation, or
order SIX HUNDRED & No/100 Dollars with interest from date until paid,
at the rate of seven per cent per annum; payable quarterly and if not so
paid to be added to the principal and thereafter bear interest at the same

74

rate, but if default be made in the payment of interest as above provided
then this note shall immediately become due and payable at the option
of the holder thereof; also to pay all legal expenses and attorney's fees
which may be incurred in the collection of this note. Both principal and
interest payable only in lawful money of the United States of America.
This note is secured by a chattel mortgage of even date herewith.

ADDRESS:_____   *(Signed)   GEO. A. HARLAN*

                                                       M. ESTHER HARLAN

And also as security for the discharge and performance of all
obligations and promises of the said Mortgagors herein contained, together
with interest thereon, and also as security for the payment by said
Mortgagors to said Mortgagee of all sums hereafter paid, laid out, ex-
pended or advanced by the said Mortgagee under the terms of this mortgage,
together with interest thereon, and also as security for the payment of
all sums which may be hereafter loaned, paid out, expended or advanced
by said Mortgagee from said Mortgagors, with interest thereon, and also as
security for the payment of any future liability or liabilities of the
Mortgagors to the Mortgagee incurred during the life of this mortgage,
with interest thereon, whether secured or unsecured, or whether said lia-
bility or liabilities shall have been created directly or indirectly with
the said mortgagee.

Said Mortgagors hereby declare and hereby warrant to the said Mortga-
gee that they are the absolute owners and in possession of all of said
mortgaged property, hereinabove described, and that the same is free and
clear of all liens, encumbrances and adverse claims whatsoever, with the
exception of the lien of this mortgage.

Said Mortgagors promise and agree to pay all taxes, assessments
and liens now subsisting or which may hereafter be imposed by national,
state, county, city or other authority upon the property hereby mortgaged,
or upon the money secured hereby, and said Mortgagors agree that said
Mortgagee may pay any suck taxes, assessments or liens without notice,
and that said Mortgagors will repay to said Mortgagee all such sums so
paid, with interest at one per cent (1%) per month, and this mortgage shall
be security for all sums so paid by said Mortgagee, together with interest
thereon, and said Mortgagee shall be the sole judge of the legality or
validity of such taxes, assessments, or liens; and said Mortgagors further
promise and agree to keep the said mortgaged property insured against
loss by fire in a sum not less than _____dollars ($____) with such in-
surance company or companies as may be approved by the Mortgagee, loss,
if any to be payable to said Mortgagee, and said policy or policies shall
be delivered to and retained by said Mortgagee. In the event that said

Mortgagors shall fail to effect and maintain such insurance the said Mortgagee may place the same at the cost and expense of said Mortgagors, and the premiums for such insurance shall be immediately repayable to the Mortgagee, together with interest thereon from the date of such payment until repaid at the rate of one per cent (1%) per month, and the cost and expenses of such insurance, together with the interest thereon, shall be secured hereby, and shall be a charge and lien against the mortgaged property.

It is hereby agreed that if the Mortgagors shall fail to make payment of any part of the principal or interest as provided in said promissory note, at the time and in the manner therein specified, or if any breach be made of any obligation or promise of the Mortgagors herein contained or hereby secured, then the whole principal sum unpaid upon said promissory note, or notes, with the interest accrued thereon, and all other sums of money due or unpaid at the time of said default, and interest thereon, or advanced under the terms of this mortgage, or secured hereby, and the interest thereon, shall immediately become due and payable at the option of the Mortgagee, without notice to the Mortgagors, and it may at once proceed to foreclose this mortgage according to law, or it may at its option, and it is hereby empowered so to do, enter upon the premises where the said mortgaged property may be and take possession thereof; and remove and sell and dispose of the same at public or private sale without any previous demand of performance or notice to the Mortgagors of any such sale whatsoever, notice of sale and demand of performance being hereby expressly waived by said mortgagors, and from the proceeds of sale retain all costs and charges incurred by it in the taking or sale of said property, including any reasonable attorney's fees incurred; also all sums due it on said promissory note, or notes, under any provisions thereof, or advanced under the terms of this mortgage, and interest thereon, or due or owing to the said Mortgagee under any provisions of this mortgage, or secured hereby, with the interest thereon, and any surplus of such proceeds remaining shall be paid to the Mortgagors, or whoever may be lawfully entitled to receive the same.

In the event that an action be brought by said Mortgagee to foreclose this mortgage there shall be due from the Mortgagors to the plaintiff therein immediately on the commencement thereof an attorney's fee of one hundred dollars ($100) in said action, and a further sum of five per cent (5%) of the amount found due, in the event that said action goes to judgment, which said sums shall be secured hereby and be made a part of said judgment, and also such further sums, if any, as said Mortgagee shall have paid for procuring an abstract of or for search of the title to said property subsequent to the execution of this mortgage, and in such suit of foreclosure the plaintiff therein shall be entitled, without notice, to the appointment of a Receiver to exercise such powers as the court shall confer. Said Mortgagors further promise and agree that they will not sell or attempt to sell said mortgaged property or remove the same from the premises on which the same is now located without the written consent of the Mortgagee.

Said Mortgagee or its agent may bid and purchase at any sale made under this mortgage or herein authorized, or at any sale made upon foreclosure of this mortgage.

Said Mortgagors further agree that if from any cause there shall be a substantial decrease in value of said mortgaged property the said Mortgagee shall have the option of demanding of said Mortgagors further security in order to offset that portion of the mortgaged property which is decreased in value, and upon the failure of said Mortgagors to give said additional security the said Mortgagee may proceed in the same manner as herein provided for any other default on the part of said Mortgagors.

IN WITNESS WHEREOF, the said mortgagors have hereunto set their hands and seals the day and year first above written.

GEO. A. HARLAN   (SEAL)

M. ESTHER HARLAN (SEAL)

STATE OF CALIFORNIA)
                 SS.   (ACKNOWLEDGEMENT)
COUNTY OF MONTEREY)

On this 2nd day of January in the year One Thousand Nine Hundred and Thirty Two before me J. W. McKINSEY, a Notary Public, in and for the County of Monterey, State of California, personally appeared GEO. A. HARLAN and M. ESTHER HARLAN known to me to be the persons whose names are subscribed to the within instrument, and acknowledged that they executed the same.

IN WITNESS WHEREOF, I have hereunto set my hand and affixed my official seal, at my office in the County of Monterey, State of California, the day and year in this certificate first above written.

J. W. McKINSEY

Notary Public in and for the County of Monterey,

State of California.

(Notary Seal),

My Commission expires July 10, 1935, __19__

STATE OF CALIFORNIA   )

                                          SS.   (MORTGAGOR'S AFFIDAVIT)

COUNTY OF MONTEREY   )

      GEO. A. HARLAN and M. ESTHER HARLAN being first duly sworn, depose and say:

That they are the Mortgagors named in the within and foregoing chattel mortgage; that the said chattel mortgage is made in good faith, and without any design to hinder, delay or defraud creditors, and that they make this affidavit for the purpose of complying with the provisions of Section 2957 of the Civil Code of the State of California relating to mortgages of personal property.

                              GEO. A. HARLAN

                              M. ESTHER HARLAN

Subscribed and sworn to before me this 2nd day of January, 1932

      J. W. McKINSEY

Notary Public in and for the County of Monterey, State of California.

      (Notarial Seal).

STATE OF CALIFORNIA   )

                                          SS. (AFFIDAVIT OF PRESIDENT OF MORTGAGEE)

COUNTY OF MONTEREY   )

      A. C. HUGHES being first duly sworn, deposes and says:

      That he is an officer, to wit, the President of MONTEREY COUNTY TRUST AND SAVINGS BANK the Mortgagee named in the within and foregoing chattel mortgage; that the said chattel mortgage is made in good faith and without any design to hinder, delay or defraud creditors, that affiant makes this affidavit as the President of said corporation, and on its behalf, and for the purpose of complying with the provisions of Section 2957 of the Civil Code of the State of California relating to mortgages or personal property.

A. C. HUGHES

*Subscribed and sworn to before
me this 4th day of January, 1932*

A. P. HOLM

*Notary Public in and for the County of
Monterey, State of California*

(Notarial Seal)

*Recorded at the Request of SALINAS TITLE GUARANTEE COMPANY JAN 4, 1932
at 39 min. past 1 P. M.......#84470......I. P."*

BALLPEIN HAMMER WITH STAR DRILL

These simple tools were the only way in which holes could be made into the solid rock for blasting with dynamite. My father spent many an hour creating the holes in the rock bluffs in Big Creek while working for the investment group. After blasting had occurred it was then necessary to break up the larger rocks with a mall and then spread the rubble to form a roadbed. My father self learned both the patience of toil and the techniques of dynamiting on this project.

THE MALL—A TOOL OF MANY USES

Next to the mattock the mall was one of the most important tools to the homesteader. It was used to force wedges into the redwood logs to make all of their building materials, such as, shakes, framing members and even the wall boards of the homestead cabins. It was used to split the pickets, slats, gates and posts used in the extensive fencing around each 160-acre plot. It was also used to reduce large rocks into small ones in the building of trails and roadways for sleds and later wagons.

H F BAR RANCH

Frank O. Horton

JOHNSON COUNTY

BUFFALO, WYOMING

Cattle and Horse
Brands

10 October 1930

Mr. George Harlan
Lucia, Monterey County
California

Dear George:

You know, we are all just poorer than the devil on account of general business conditions; so don't want to spend one penny that isn't absolutely necessary until after the first of the new year.

Therefore we will call off all work that we had in mind until I see you in California early in December.

I have had the Chicago office mail direct to Mr. Henderson a check for $75.00, which he undoubtedly has by now.

I have also written Marion telling him that Barney was probably eating his head off and therefore needed a lot of riding and therefore to use him in connection with the water measurements which he is taking.

Very best regards to all of you,

Yours sincerely,

Franl O Horton

FOH:RRM

COPY OF THE LETTER SENT TO MY FATHER EXPLAINING THE SHORTAGE OF CASH CAUSED BY THE DEPRESSED ECONOMY

The sale of the Big Creek property to Edward S. Moore, and many other parcels in the area, subsequently brought about the large expansion of my father's cattle raising endeavors.

George and Esther experienced hardships in the depression years of 1929 through 1933. Livestock prices plummeted, and they still owed money on the ranch. Only by extra work were they able to clear their debts and pay off their loan. My mother said that the small sum she received from teaching made the difference.

My first memories were those of my father and mother working from before daylight to well after dark just to keep things going. My father had gone to Redwood School with no shoes because his parents could not afford them in 1898. I remember that my shoes were badly worn, with holes, in 1932, but still I was never without shoes. My cousins came to school with sections of old car tires nailed to the soles of their shoes. Times were difficult but, because we lived on the ranch, we all had sufficient food. We always had a surplus of butter, eggs, milk, cream and vegetables. We could not afford to kill our livestock for food because they were our cash crop. Any cattle or pigs that we had for sale were driven 50 miles to market in King City, and there they brought a price as low as six cents per pound.

My mother sold eggs for twelve cents a dozen, and she sold butter for twenty-five cents a pound. As small children my brother, Donald, and I churned the cream into butter by cranking a handle on a machine designed for that purpose. The churn consisted of a tapered square metal frame which contained a place to secure the square (tinned steel) container of cream (which held about three gallons) with a drain pipe and cap near the bottom. A right-angle gear mechanism at the top caused a steel shaft (also tinned), with a four bladed wooden paddle attached, to rotate within the reservoir of cream as the crank handle was turned. The top of the cream container was lidded with two rectangular wooden pieces notched to fit closely around the rotating shaft and rabbeted around three edges to fit part way down into the square container. Each lid had a small wooden knob attached so a lid may be lifted for inspection inside the container. Sometimes the butter would "come" quickly and other times it seemed to take an eternity.

Once the butter was churned, my mother would spend another half hour draining off the butter milk (for pig feed) and then washing the butter repeatedly in cold water. Each washing required thorough "working" of the butter with a wooden paddle to get out all of the trapped butter milk. After this operation she added salt to the butter and again "worked" it with the wooden paddle until it was evenly distributed throughout the butter. In the summer and fall months (when green grass was not a part of the cow's diet) she also added food coloring along with the salt to give the butter the typical yellow appearance. She then formed the butter into one-pound blocks by pressing the butter into a wooden mold equipped with a "pusher" to force out the formed butter "block" onto a piece of special "butter paper". Upon wrapping in butter paper it was then placed in a waxed box designed especially for that purpose. The butter paper and butter boxes were ordered from the Montgomery Ward catalog and delivered by mail to our house.

Due to a drought condition during the winter of 1932-1933, and also the following year, my father had to carry hay on horseback to his starving cattle just to keep them alive. During the summer, he had to clean out the watering holes almost daily to give the animals a place to drink. The natural springs were low on water flow and, at best, they were equipped with hand hewn redwood log troughs that held only enough water for a single cow. The cattle would spend most of the day standing in the muddy areas around the springs trying to drink from hoof imprints to get survival water. Later on, as we grew older, we acquired and placed used cast iron bath tubs at these spring locations for much more adequate watering of the cattle and other animals.

During the period of time that the three of us boys grew up at the ranch my father maintained a number of horses and mules. Our favorite horse was named Babe. She was very gentle and never balked at the various tasks that she was to perform. My mother, who was our teacher, usually rode Babe to the school house in our early years when Redwood School was located in Section 8. We kids would hold onto Babe's tail and get a much-needed boost as we walked up the hill. The school was over a mile away and over 1,500 feet higher in elevation than our house. She was called upon to drag lilac trees (cyanosis) to the house for firewood from distant locations. Babe was always preferred to work as a one-horse team, since she could be led through very irregular terrain. Pulling a spring tooth through recently burned ground where barley had been planted was a chore she excelled at. Sledding household furniture such as stoves, water heaters, school desks, water tank materials or pipe were other tasks she was called upon to do. She also hauled sand from the beach for our cement work and posts, poles and pickets from the creek to our fences at all locations on the ranch.

We had two mules, Big Jack and Little Jack and they usually pastured with the other horses. They were used, along with other horses and mules, for hauling mail from Jolon to the coast when my father held a contract to deliver mail from 1920 to 1932. They were also used to sled boulders from the fields to the ocean bank as my father persisted in clearing the fields of the unwanted obstructions. I remember seeing the two mules pulling a fully loaded sled of large rocks. Little Jack, though smaller, always worked beyond his potential to keep up to his team mate. Big Jack

DONALD, GENE AND STANLEY ON BABE AT THE
GEORGE AND ESTHER HARLAN RANCH

Babe was our most trusted horse while the three of us kids were growing up. She was very gentle and seemed to understand the tasks that she was asked to accomplish. On the way to school (my mother usually rode Babe) Donald and I walked behind, holding onto her tail, to give us an extra boost going up the steep hill. At times she would stop to rest and we (not paying attention) would walk right up between her hind legs without serious consequences.

AN EXAMPLE OF AN OLD (PARTLY ROTTED) PIG FEED TROUGH
MADE FROM A REDWOOD LOG BY HOLLOWING OUT
THE CENTER PORTION WITH AN AXE OR AN ADZ

This technique was also used to make water troughs and cattle feed troughs. Even a large diameter log could not hold sufficient water at the natural springs for cattle to satisfy their thirst quickly. They consequently spent much of their day sipping from hoof depressions in the mud surrounding the spring

A WOODEN MOCK-UP SHOWING HOW A HORSESHOE IS ATTACHED TO A HORSE'S HOOF

The nails used in this mock-up were oversized for the shoe being demonstrated. The nail head should fit all the way down into the groove in the horseshoe. The mock-up demonstrates quite clearly how the nails are bent over or "clenched" to the horse's hoof. It becomes obvious that each horse required a different size of shoe and had to be fitted by forging to its proper application. Nails also came in different sizes and were selected for the shoe size.

was usually part of a two-horse team that pulled the side hill plow, the spring tooth, the harrow, the mowing machine, the hay rake and the hay sled or hay wagon.

My father was quite skillful in putting new shoes on all of the horses and mules. Among his many learned skills, he was an accomplished farrier as well. He purchased the steel shoes in the rough in a size corresponding to the particular horse being shoed. He then used a coal fired forge to heat the shoes to a red-hot condition for forming on an anvil to the exact shape of the hoof being shoed. I remember the mules had much smaller hoofs than the horses and required a unique shape as well. The old worn out shoes were removed by clipping the clenched ends of the horseshoe nails at the side of the hoof with a pair of end nippers, then, he would use the nippers between the shoe and the hoof surface to "lift" off the worn-out old shoe. He would remove excess hoof material at the toe and flatten the bottom of the hoof with a rasp in preparation for attaching the new shoe. The new shoe, very hot, was placed against the hoof surface to "burn in" a perfect fit to the animal's hoof. The new shoe was cooled in water, then, it was nailed in place with the special horse shoe nails of the right size. There were about four nails on each side of the shoe for a total of eight nails for each of the horse's feet. The nails were designed to exit the hoof on the side in the "dead" hoof material. The ends were then nipped off about a quarter inch outside the hoof and clenched (bent downward) to keep the nail from loosening. All of these operations required the cooperation of the animal being shoed. The front leg was bent at the knee and the hoof was held between my father's legs exposing the bottom of the foot. The rear foot was lifted to the rear and the ankle was bent sharply between my father's legs to expose the bottom of the rear hoof. Neither of these positions was "safe" for the horse shoer and much trust between the horse or mule and my father was required. If the animal was not cooperative, and resisted the shoeing operation, a person could be seriously hurt as a result. Teaching a young horse to accept this procedure took many hours of training.

The plowing of the chosen fields for raising red oat hay was usually started in late February. My father used a two-horse team to pull the side hill plow. He would get up at the break of day to do his milking, then, he would immediately start the plowing after a 7 AM breakfast. The plowing progressed, one furrow at a time, throughout the morning and afternoon hours with only a short break for lunch. My father walked every step of the way behind the plow, in the furrow just created, with the reins of the horses over his shoulder and both hands on the handles of the plow. He strained to guide the plow, in an effort to miss obstructions (usually rocks that were still in the field), which required great physical strength.

Toward 5 PM he unharnessed the team, washed them down, doctored any abrasions and then put them out to pasture, only to follow with the evening milking chores. It took nearly a week to plow the 10 to 15 acres of land that were typically used for growing hay. The whole process was usually interrupted by a broken leather "tug", single tree or double tree as a result of the plow hitting an unseen rock. To fix the broken equipment he would "patch" the tug by riveting in overlapping layers of leather. To fix the single or doubletrees he had to take a trip up the mountain to get a special kind of oak (valpariso), that was exceptionally strong, and whittle it into the shape of the broken member and transfer the metal parts from the old to the new. The plow also required a new landslide (shoe) and plowshare every so often due to wear. When the plowing was completed he hand sowed (broadcast) the seed grain onto the field and then immediately followed with a one-horse team and a pair of harrows to cover the seed.

We also had a horse called Wyoming and another called Trixie in the early years. Later we had a horse named Pink (she was roan in color) that was gentle but, at the same time, unpredictable. She shied at any machinery or loud noises and I experienced a "pitch-off" when riding her near the highway as a greyhound bus passed by. She always shirked her duties when she was teamed up with any of the other horses. The "double trees" were never square with the load that was being pulled by her and another one of our steeds. After the neighbor, Edward S. Moore, sold out to John Nesbitt we added another horse named Sleepy (a gelding) to our group. He was similar to Babe in his mannerisms and performed well at most of the tasks on the ranch.

My father also had a special stallion named Bunch. He was used for most of the cattle work that my father did on the open range. He could not be trusted with other horses, so he was kept in a special pasture that we called The Ranchito Field. This was some distance from our house and it was our duty on many occasions to either get him for my father's use or deliver him back to his pasture after my father had finished for the day with him. He never kicked or bit us but he regularly tried to push us off his back against some trail side tree along the way. We learned to hold our leg up on the side where the tree was located and he simply scrubbed his ribs as he passed by. Sadly, he escaped from his pasture through an open gate that a trespassing hunter had neglected to close and joined the rest of the horses one day in the early 1940s. He aggressively pushed and bit the other animals mercilessly. He pushed Babe into a three-inch diameter broken tree limb that penetrated into her flesh and rib cage breaking her shoulder. She consequently fell into a rough portion of the creek where we found her later that day. There was no hope of saving Babe so my father, using the only tool he had, swung the mattock blade to

FARMERS MERCANTILE CO.

GROCERIES AND HARDWARE

IMPLEMENTS & TRACTORS

Salinas, California

Sold to   Mr. G. Harlan.

LUCIA, VIA SAN SIMEON,
California.

1931

Jan	10	2 52 G Chilled Shares @ 1.65		3	30
		Landside F 454		1	50
				4	80

PAID

FEB 2 1931

FARMERS MERCANTILE CO.

By _M.E.R._

Thank you.

COPY OF BILLING FROM FAMERS MERCANTILE CO. IN SALINAS
FOR SIDEHILL PLOW PARTS

My father would use the party telephone line through King City to place his order with the above merchant. The two "chilled shares" meant plow shares made of carbon steel and cooled quickly in cold water to create hardness in the steel. The plow share was located at the front of the plow and initiated the cut of the furrow. It was exposed to much friction against the soil and rocks which caused noticeable wear and need for replacement. The landslide or shoe was a part of the plow that slid along the bottom of the furrow supporting the weight of the plow and also experienced noticeable wear. The date of the billing indicates my father was preparing for the 1931 plowing season.

AN OLD ORIGINAL SINGLE TREE

This example shows how the wood will weaken with age and not hold up to the strain of a horse pulling a load. My father selected a special variety of oak that grew at the higher elevations to renew a broken single tree. Note the special shape of the hooks where the tugs attached. My father sometimes had to forge these metal parts, as well, using a coal fired forge and hammer and anvil. This was another skill that he learned in his ranching endeavors.

MOWING MACHINE USED AT LOPEZ POINT

This mowing machine was horse drawn by a team of two horses. Power to operate the sickle bar (here shown in the upright position) was delivered from the wheels of the machine through a gear box and drive shaft to the pitman arm, which, in turn, moved the sickle back and forth as the machine moved forward. The sickle blades were triangular in shape and had serrations along their edges. The sickle blades were riveted onto the sickle bar and required re-sharpening quite frequently and sometimes replacement. My father learned to do all of these tasks as the need arose.

HORSE DRAWN HAY RAKE USED BY MY FATHER

This machine was also pulled by a two-horse team. It was used to gather the hay, after it had been cut a few inches above the ground with the mowing machine, into windrows for preliminary drying in the sun. My father rode the machine in the steel formed seat and directed the team with the reins of the harness. He also used his hands and feet at the right moment to cause the rake teeth to "trip" and leave the gathered hay at the right spot. The tripping action was driven by a cog on the wheel hub that, in turn, caused the shaft, which held the rake teeth, to rotate part of a turn and consequently lift the teeth free of the load it had collected.

GEORGE AND ESTHER HARLAN'S HORSE DRAWN WAGON
AT THE HARLAN RANCH
Circa 1928

A load of hay has just been deposited in the barn on the left. Marian Smith, an itinerate named Scow, Gene and George Harlan are in the wagon and are headed to the field to bring in another load of hay. Donald is standing along side of the wagon taking in the activities. Dixie, the dog, and Trixie, the horse, are seen on the right. The other horse of the team is obscured behind Trixie. The chicken house, pig shed and granary are visible in the background.

The wagon was the next step up from the go-devil as a conveyance to haul hay and other materials for the Harlan family at their ranch. As we, the Harlan boys, grew older the hauling of hay became a regular summer task for us all. The barn would normally hold all of the hay from a selected field that had been planted that year. A good crop of hay meant stuffing the last load into the highest peak of the roof line.

her forehead. I recall the cutting blade of the mattock penetrated 5 or 6 inches into her head and brain, causing her immediate death. Though her death was instantaneous, the memories of that day will not leave me until I die. I often wonder how my father was strong enough to carry out the necessary act, and how he later lived with the memory for years to come.

Ranching is not an easy profession for the weak hearted. We lost many of our animals over the years when they were pushed by others or slipped and fell off the ocean bank. We made many gallant efforts to dig an escape trail back to the safety of the field if the animal did not suffer broken limbs. Sometimes we succeeded and other times we did not. For those who did suffer broken limbs we were forced to shoot them and put them out of their misery. There were animals that slipped and fell into remote ditches in the back country and would suffer the same end, if not starvation, as described above. In more than one case cows were bit by rattlesnakes on their neck and tongue causing exceptional swelling and near loss of life. Occasionally deer hunters would intentionally shoot at our animals with rifles at night time with the aid of spot lights from the highway, in an illegal attempt to bag a deer or simply to retaliate for not allowing them to hunt on our property. At other times trespassers would cut the wire fencing and allow animals to access the highway where they inevitably caused an accident with a passing vehicle.

The California Fish and Game Commission saw fit to transfer problem black bears from Yosemite and other parts of the State to the Santa Lucia Mountains a number of times over the years. The ranchers were not informed of this action and only learned of it when they experienced losses of calves and other farm animals. One such animal attacked a calf in the open field in daylight hours inshore from Lopez Rock. The attack was witnessed by members of the highway maintenance crew and their actions, along with the defensive actions of the resident bull and cows discouraged the bear from completing his aggression. The calf, however, was knocked senseless and required constant in corral care and never did recover from its injuries.

There were always the opportunistic coyotes and mountain lions that would take advantage of a newborn calf. We had examples of mountain lions killing calves weighing as much as 3 to 4 hundred pounds. In the early years the State of California offered a bounty on mountain lions and the numbers were kept in check by local hunters who maintained two or three hounds and made a meager living collecting lion bounties. Steve Avila; son of Juan Bautista Avila, one of the local early homesteaders; did this for a number of years. I personally trapped dozens of coyotes in an effort to keep their numbers in check. Our ranch was noted for its

GEORGE HARLAN WITH HIS TEAM OF SLEEPY AND PINK

This is one of the last times that our horses were used for labors on the ranch. The picture was taken in the late 1940's when machinery was replacing our older methods. Close inspection shows the harness, double trees, single trees and spring tooth harrow being pulled through the recently plowed soil.

ADA SMITH ON BUNCH NEAR THE GEORGE AND ESTHER HARLAN
HOME WITH TAG IN THE FOREGROUND AND GENE VISIBLE IN THE
BACKGROUND

This horse was used by my father regularly to work with his range cattle. George usually carried a machete in a scabbard on the saddle to cut hanging branches of trees and brush over the many trails he traveled. A small mattock was also strapped to the saddle for digging out springs and creating clean water holes for the cattle. He also carried his 22 special pistol or 22 special rifle on the saddle as well. Bunch also carried survival supplies of hay and cotton cake to the cattle in need during drought years.

THE FIRST AND MOST IMPORTANT TOOL OF THE BIG SUR HOMESTEADERS—THE MATTOCK

The Harlans learned to swing the mattock at an early age. Clearing the land of brush to create grassland was primary to the success of every homesteader. The mattock was a very versatile hand tool. It could be used to grub brush and cut the roots of the greasewood, skunk berry and lilac with moderate effort. It could be used to clean the springs for the cattle and loosen the soil for planting in the home garden. It could be used to remove the head of a rattlesnake and even, as I fatefully learned, dispatch our favorite horse.

profusion of wildlife with "common sense" predator control. Any relaxing of these controls immediately created losses that brought about the collapse of the ranching business and eventually the loss of game animals and even household pets.

In addition to his large herd of range stock my father maintained a few head of dairy cows from the early 1940's until he died in 1985. He milked a few of them every night and morning by hand and provided our household with fresh whole milk, cream and butter. He also maintained a flock of chickens which produced fresh eggs as well. During the late 1940's, 1950's and 1960's he supplied neighbors with these items on a regular basis.

My mother kept records of the items sent to each of these neighbors, and a small charge was made for them. The Kenworthy's, who lived near Lucia, were supplied with 12 pounds of butter, 10 gallons of milk and 17 dozen eggs for the month of June in 1949. During that same month the Fifes, who lived on Point "16", were provided with 18 pounds of butter, 29 gallons of milk, 20 dozen eggs and 10 pints of cream. The Houks, who lived in our old house, in the 1950's and 60's were also supplied these items as well. Prices ranged from 35 cents a pint for cream, 40 cents per gallon of milk, 50 cents per pound of butter and 55 cents per dozen of eggs.

Over the years my father experimented with various breeds of dairy cows for his milking herd. He started with Short Horns in the 1930's, Red Poled in the early 1940's, Guernseys and Jerseys in the 40's and 50's, and the most successfully, Brown Swiss in the 1960's. He did not like the Short Horns because they had horns that curved inward and he was afraid the horns could injure other animals. The Red Poled from Argentina had no horns, but they were large boned and did not produce milk in sufficient quantity. Our Red Poled bull was very good natured but his offspring had a habit of "going wild" easily and were difficult to round up from the range. The Guernseys were good milkers but had to be dehorned and did not "fit in" with the rest of the herd to well. One Guernsey bull calf that we raised turned into a mean and aggressive animal that we could not keep. The Jerseys were a small animal, gave rich milk, but not in any great quantity. The Brown Swiss turned out to be very well suited to our needs. They were gentle natured, of good size, and mixed "bred" well with the Angus beef breeds that we ranged on the ranch as a whole. The brown hair of our later Black Angus was a genetic throwback to the Brown Swiss breed.

Though my father did most of the milking, separating the cream from the milk and washing up the milking utensils each morning and evening, my mother was very

DONALD HARLAN AND HIS DOG, SHEP, WITH A MOUNTAIN
LION THAT SHEP CORNERED UNDER A GREASEWOOD

This was in the early 1940's when no controls existed on lion hunting. In fact, there was a State bounty offered in an effective effort to control the number of mountain lions in the State. Since later controls have been established by poorly informed legislators the mountain lion population has exploded to the point where they are starving to death for lack of food. They have put cattle ranching out of business at Lopez Point. They have eaten nearly all of the deer and many of the other animals. They are currently a threat to household pets and even human beings.

STEVE AVILA AND TONY FONTES IN THE 1930'S

Steve Avila, son of Juan Bautista Avila, an early Santa Lucia pioneer, was a noted mountain lion hunter. When ranch livestock were killed by a lion Steve would be notified of the occurrence, and in a few hours, he would be on the scene. He maintained a couple of bloodhounds which tracked the lion after a kill until they treed it. A wise lion might travel many miles before treeing, but the bloodhounds never would give up. Steve would then kill the lion and collect the State bounty. He made a meager living at the trade. Tony was a caretaker for George Gamboa and broke horses for riding and shoeing. Tony was a frequent helper for my father in rodeo activities. They both knew their trades well.

involved in churning, washing and salting and coloring and packing the butter in cartons, washing and candling the eggs and placing them in cartons, as well as, keeping the records of those items sent to the neighbors.

The three of us boys also shared many of the labors described above. We were especially talented in churning the cream into butter. My mother would pour in about a gallon and a half of cream into the churn, then, we turned the handle of the churn for as long as it took to bring about the separation of butter from the buttermilk. Sometimes it only took a few minutes and other times it took nearly an hour. Over hundreds of churnings we could never quite figure out why the time, it took to make butter, varied so much.

Construction of the work road through our property, in 1933, brought about many changes for all of us. We felt much like the Indians must have felt when the white men first arrived off our coast a few centuries earlier. My father had agreed with the highway engineers to donate his land for the highway right of way "if" they would locate the highway at the extreme upper edge of his fields; to relocate a number of his buildings that would be destroyed within the right of way; to provide three underpasses for his cattle, and possibly vehicles as well; to clear all of his fields of debris (rocks, etc.) that the construction may create; and to pay for the construction of livestock fencing on both sides of the right of way.

The first condition was not met and the highway ended up consuming much of the nearly level ground of the fields. My father brought suit against the State of California and after many years of court appearances and stomach ulcers, a settlement was arrived at. The highway construction went ahead as the engineers had planned it, however, and it left a bad feeling with my father and mother.

All of the other conditions were met, however, and I remember clearly the activities which took place on our ranch in 1932 through 1938. Convicts were used for most of the hand labor involved in the highway construction. A group of convicts came through first, with a foreman, to clear and dig an access trail by hand on grade with the new highway. In some places this trail was cut through almost vertical slopes. Soon after the trail passed through our property a moderate size Loraine steam shovel, operated by a Mr. Henderson, cut a work road through on the same route as the trail. It went right below our granary and right through our pig pens and chicken pens in the summer of 1933. Our split redwood barn was still intact below the highway. Convicts rebuilt the chicken house above our home, away from the highway right of way.

A GUERNSEY-JERSEY MIX MILK COW WITH HER CALF AT THE HARLAN RANCH AT LOPEZ POINT
Early 1950's

This is an example of the dairy breed experiment that my father performed over the years. This particular cow had been bred by the registered Aberdeen Angus bull. The offspring, as seen here, has the coloring of his mother but the thick body and short legs of the Angus breed. The Guernsey offspring, though gentle, had a tendency to become very head strong and difficult to handle. They would likely run right over a person who was trying to direct them into a corral or some other location they didn't particularly like. Note the cow's ear marking of the Harlan registered brand.

HAND CRANK CREAM SEPARATOR USED BY GEORGE HARLAN

My father turned the crank on this machine many hundreds of thousands of turns to produce the cream that he sold during World War II years. I helped with the milking of as many as 32 cows, each morning and evening, taking the milk from the right side of the cow and letting the calf have the left side during this time.

A BUTTER CHURN VERY SIMILAR TO THE ONE THE
HARLAN'S USED FOR MANY YEARS ON THEIR RANCH

Soon after the work road was constructed, a large P & H steam shovel followed making the highway to its full width. This second shovel loaded most of the diggings onto dump trucks which made short hauls to adjacent canyons that were spanned with fill dirt and rocks over culverts. This large steam shovel did most of the work, but it required the use of much black powder and dynamite blasts to loosen the material so it could dig it efficiently.

In preparation for the "blasts", as we called them, convicts made "coyote and bootleg" holes by hand or with compressed air operated drills. These holes were then packed with a combination of black powder and dynamite and interconnected with electric blasting caps. The steam shovel would stop, not far from the blast sight, and swing its bucket in the opposite direction of the blast location. The convicts and operators would get inside the bucket with the ignition device and push down on the plunger.

Dynamite was delivered to the convicts for setting each charge in 25 or 50-pound wooden boxes, and black powder was delivered in 30-pound corrugated steel cans. The 50-pound wooden boxes became a popular item with all of the families that lived nearby. They were constructed of a top-quality pine lumber with square dovetail joints where the ends joined the sides. The tops and bottoms were nailed onto the sides and ends with four penny nails. The empty boxes were used for storage and shelving in many of the homes. The steel cans which had contained

the black powder were painted black on the outside and were equipped with a small round push-in lid. They readily rusted, and, because of the small opening, they were almost useless for any practical purpose.

An interesting sidelight to the highway construction was observing the gathering convict work crew for the day standing in a group throwing sticks of dynamite onto a fire to take the chill out of the air. The dynamite burned vigorously but never caused an explosion. The same could not be said for the black powder. It exploded from the smallest of sparks.

We were going to Redwood Branch School in our own home that year and I remember the intentional blasts were sometimes spectacular. It was difficult for us students to sit in class quietly with rocks falling around the house and on the roof. We lost some shingles that my father had to replace, but surprisingly no one was ever injured. The railing on our front porch, which my father had made of natural round limbs set into round holes bored into the top and bottom rails, sustained the most damage. It took a couple of direct hits with moderate damage.

P & H STEAM SHOVEL CLEARING A SLIDE ON HIGHWAY 1

Location was south of Gorda circa 1935. The P & H, operated by a Mr. Jones and oiled by a Mr. Burris, was the largest of the three shovels that worked on the south half of Highway 1. It did the widening from a work road to full width. It loaded the dump trucks for building all of the fill areas over underground culverts in ravines where bridges were not built. Its bucket held approximately three cubic yards of material. The bucket served as a safe haven for the operators when blasts were set off. On weekends when the shovel was idle my brother and I regularly sat in this bucket using nails between our fingers for gear shift levers and our imagination to engineer our own highway.

A third steam shovel, a moderate size Lima, operated by a Mr. Paulson and oiled by a Mr. Brockelbank, came through after the P & H to dress up the irregularities and to remove the tailings that the convicts created as they "sloped" the high cut banks by hand.

These steam shovels were a marvel to all who lived on the coast, both young and old. We all had learned to work by hand to grub brush, dig trails, create excavations, till soil, develop water spring sources, remove boulders from tilled fields, etc. These jobs were all done with the most meager tools, such as axe, mattock, pick, shovel, crowbar, buck saw, maul and other such hand tools. To see these monsters rip through rock, soil, and tree stumps, as though it were child's play impressed us all. My grandfather, Wilber Harlan, would sit on a hill near the construction site and watch in awe for hours on end. Even though he was quite well read and self-educated, he never could get his fill of observing these massive machines. Much the same could have been said about the rest of us, if we could have taken the time from other activities to do the same.

Through all of this my mother seemed most concerned about our whereabouts in relation to the convicts. In actuality, most of the convicts were quite caring for our safety, and on a number of occasions, when I was with my father, they carried me across muddy slide areas so I wouldn't get my shoes or clothes dirty.

The convicts were confined to camp locations over night, but on weekends when they were off duty, they would sometimes come to our ranch and fish or harvest abalones from our beach. My father was somewhat concerned because of the extreme number they were taking. Their interest was both in eating the fish and making artifacts from the shells of the abalone in their free time. In spite of the convicts, the Japanese divers and the tremendous loss of abalone due to sand and mud suffocation, they survived in goodly numbers. A few years later, the sea otters were far more of a hazard to the abalone. In just 5 years between 1942 and 1947, the otters made a clean sweep of the abalone population.

The thirties were full of change. Looking back on those years, now, it is hard to believe that we came through it all as well as we did. Though my father's mail contract ended in 1932, he took on extensive new responsibilities.

In addition to Esther and George's own acreage my father leased Forest Service land in the adjacent township in the head of Big Creek to range a few head of cattle during the summer and fall months. Looking after these cattle in rough country was not an easy chore. He would saddle up his horse, Bunch, and with his dog,

A BLASTING POWDER BOX[4] SIMILAR TO THE ONES USED ON THE CONSTRUCTION OF HIGHWAY ONE ON THE BIG SUR COAST

Thousands upon thousands of these boxes were used to deliver the dynamite necessary for the construction of Highway One in the early 1930's. The empty boxes were used for early morning fires by the convicts to warm up before going to work. When there were no old boxes available they also used the sticks of dynamite for firewood as well. The empty boxes were also used by the employees and local people for furniture in their homes. They were stacked on their sides against a wall creating a very usable set of shelving.

HARRY HICKS AND WILBER JUDSON HARLAN WATCHING A STEAM
SHOVEL WORKING ON HIGHWAY 1

This picture, taken in early 1934 from a location near Rigdon Memorial Fountain, shows the highway work road nearing completion. This shovel pictured was working from the south toward a similar shovel working from the north toward their meeting point about ½ mile south of Big Creek. The other shovel can just be seen as a light spot in the distance on the right.

At this time the work road to the south was being used by locals for their first automobile connection to the outer world via San Simeon, Morrow Bay and San Luis Obispo. Harry Hicks, a nephew of Wilber Harlan, had driven with his family to the Harlan ranch in his automobile. The last access road to the ranch from Highway One was made by Fred and Marion Harlan with a sidehill plow, a Fresno scraper and a team of horses. Edward S. Moore work crews were being supplied by trucks to construct the Moore mansion on Point 16 at this time as well.

Sport would spend most of the day travelling to this grazing area to check on water sources for his cattle. In summer months some of the natural springs would dry up or produce very low flows. George carried a few tools on his saddle to aid in creating better basins for cattle and other animals to drink at these springs.

In the late 1920's and early 1930's a famed person named Miss Marion Hollins (who acted as a real estate broker) bought up most of the land surrounding the Wilber and George Harlan properties to form what was known as The Santa Lucia Corporation. These homestead properties included the Gamboas, the Borondas, the Avilas, the Danis, the Dolans, the Brunnettis and the recently defaulted Warren Gorrell, Frank O. Horton and John Marble holdings. This combined property totaled nearly 10,000 acres. Miss Hollins was in contact with a wealthy person, Edward Small Moore, during this land acquisition action and was financed by him. The land was eventually bought by Mr. Moore in its entirety and the property became known as Circle "M" Ranch.

The new owner, Edward S. Moore, offered a contract to my father to graze cattle on their land if he would pay them one fourth of the net profits from the cattle sales, and to supply them with a butchered steer every two weeks. The range for grazing increased from roughly 300 to 6,000 acres when this agreement was made. It took almost three years to save enough young animals to stock this acreage. My father was a master at raising cattle, and he was able to live up to his agreements quite well.

Butchering a steer weighing 800 to 900 pounds on the hoof was no easy task. We had no facilities to carry out this process efficiently when we started. My father and my two brothers selected a site in the Ranchito Creek, where a large redwood tree had a natural horizontal limb about 20 feet off of the ground. From this limb they suspended two sets of (4 to 1) block and tackle spaced about three feet apart. About an hour and a half before sunset (so flies would not be a problem) my father would kill the selected animal, with his Winchester 22 Special rifle, by carefully placing one shot to the brain. After bleeding the animal we would roll it onto a sled and have Babe (our very trustworthy horse) pull it to the slaughtering tree. There we would carefully skin the rear legs down far enough to allow hooking the lower tackle blocks into the natural tendon space just above the "rear knee". From this point we would pull each block upward until the head just cleared the ground. We would continue skinning down to the ears then remove the head with the skin attached. We would then slit the carcass from top to bottom on the belly side through the soft tissue, then being very careful to split the pelvic bone and the brisket bone in the exact center, thereby allowing the removal of all the internal organs. We would carefully save the liver, the heart, the sweet breads, the tongue, muscle from the jowls and the muscle connecting the rib cage to the abdomen (commonly called skirt or slaughterhouse steak) for our own use. The lungs and kidneys were usually fed to our dogs and the rest of the offal was disposed of by our pigs. When removing the tongue and jowl flesh we would also separate the head from the skin then hang the skin over a drying rack. The carcass would be pulled higher for overnight cooling so wild animals could not reach it. Then, the next morning my father would quarter the carcass, place each quarter in a clean white sack (mattress cover) and load it into his car for delivery to the Moore ranch walk-in refrigerator. There were a number of employees at the ranch headquarters that consumed this beef in the two-week period.

In 1935, my father took on the job of building the new school at a site on my Aunt Lulu's homestead about a mile east of our ranch house. He, with some help from Gene, my brother, and Ernest Straight Delvey, his brother-in-law, worked diligently to get the new structure completed in time for the influx of students that occurred during the highway and bridge construction in the mid to late 1930s. When the structure was completed George transported all of the furniture and books to the new site by pack mule and other means. The rows of desks were pulled by our horse, Babe, down the mile-long mountain trail, like a sled on the wooden runners which the desks were attached to. In many tight places the outboard support for the row of desks skidded along on the top of brush below the trail. The desk frames (made of cast iron) and many of the other items were very fragile and it was amazing that nothing was damaged or broken in transit. I would say it was a tribute to Babe and her very wise and cooperative ways.

My mother was one of forty teachers to teach at Redwood School in the span of 62 years (1880 to 1942). Most of the teachers taught for two years or less, but my mother taught for over 16 years.

Teaching at the new school house was a pleasure for my mother. There were six students (all brothers, sisters or cousins to one another) during the first year (1936-1937). We all got along well together and my mother seemed to enjoy the new surroundings with adequate storage room for teaching supplies, and other conveniences that she did not have in the cramped quarters of our old house.

As our teacher, my mother went out of her way to explore things that were undoubtedly very interesting to her, and at the same time whetting our interests in various subjects as students. She would gather a group of us after dark and take us on walks along the newly constructed highway to observe the planets, the moon,

Form 656
Revised Jan., 1931

GRAZING PERMIT
10-YEAR, ANNUAL, SHORT SEASON, OR TEMPORARY

(This permit can not be transferred or renewed except in accordance with the regulations of the Secretary of Agriculture)

(Right.)   (Left.)

SHEEP
Brand

April 1, 1935
(Date)

Geo. A. Harlan,
(Name of permittee)

San Simeon, California
(Post office address)

DEAR SIR:

Subject to payment of all fees required by the regulations of the Secretary of Agriculture governing grazing on the National Forests, you are hereby authorized to pasture on lands of the United States

in the ___Santa Barbara___ National Forest, within the area described below, or as modified in accordance with the regulations of the Secretary of Agriculture, during the period specified in the letter of transmittal approving your application, the number and class of stock stated in the letter of transmittal furnished you each year by the Forest Supervisor, which when received back by you, stamped "Paid," shall validate this permit for the time stated in said letter and become a part thereof. This permission, however, to become null and void immediately upon your failure to pay promptly any such fees when due or upon any violation of the terms of your application or of this permit, including the stipulations on the back hereof, or of the provisions of any such letter of transmittal or of said regulations, or in the event said lands shall be eliminated from said National Forest.

Eight head of cattle to graze under temporary permit from March 16, 1935 to
(Description of area covered by permit)

October 15, 1935, on SE¼ Section 29, T 21 S, R. 4 E., and SW¼ of NW¼ of

Section 28, T 21 S, R 4 E, M.D.M., Monterey District.

C. B. Robinson
Acting   Forest Supervisor.

c8—5101

COPY OF FOREST SERVICE GRAZING PERMIT
FOR THE SUMMER OF 1935

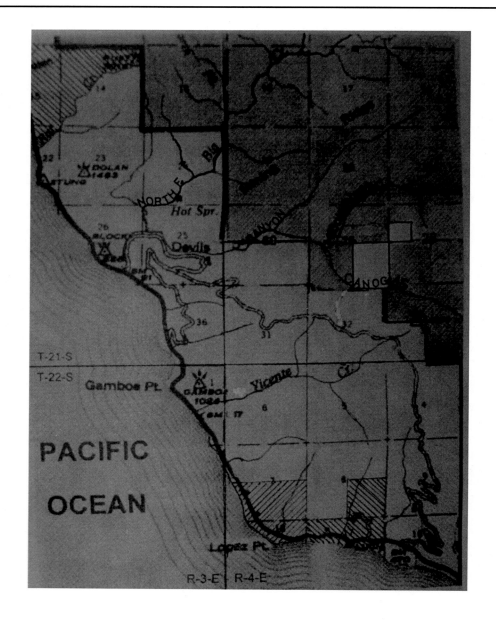

MAP OF GEORGE AND ESTHER HARLAN GRAZING LANDS
OVER AN EXTENDED PERIOD OF TIME

Harlan cattle grazed on nearly 8,000 acres including all light shaded areas excepting the two areas with left-hand hatching near Rat Canyon on the northwest and portions of section 8 and 17 which was Wilber Harlan's ranch. The right-hand hatching is of the home ranch of George and Esther Harlan.

the stars and other wonders of the heavens. She was especially attracted to Venus which appeared very bright in the western sky after dark at certain times of the year. I think she was especially interested in Venus because, at that time, scientists thought our nearest neighboring planet may actually have life on it similar to the Earth. We did not have access to telescopes, but with our old pair of binoculars, held very carefully, we could observe the crescent shape of Venus at these times. These outings generated a lifetime interest in the heavens for me and my two brothers. My older brother, Gene, became an assistant astronomer for the University of California at Lick Observatory on Mt. Hamilton. While there he discovered a long period comet (Comet Harlan 1976g), which was named after him.

My mother was one of forty teachers to teach at Redwood School in the span of 62 years (1880 to 1942). Most of the teachers taught for two years or less, but my mother taught for over 16 years. Teaching at the new school house was a pleasure for my mother. There were six students (all brothers, sisters or cousins to one another) during the first year (1936-1937). We all got along well together and my mother seemed to enjoy the new surroundings with adequate storage room for teaching supplies, and other conveniences that she did not have in the cramped quarters of our old house.

As our teacher, my mother, went out of her way to explore things that were undoubtedly very interesting to her, and at the same time whetting our interests in various subjects as students. She would gather a group of us after dark and take us on walks along the newly constructed highway to observe the planets, the moon, the stars and other wonders of the heavens. She was especially attracted to Venus which appeared very bright in the western sky after dark at certain times of the year. I think she was especially interested in Venus because, at that time, scientists thought our nearest neighboring planet may actually have life on it similar to the Earth. We did not have access to telescopes, but with our old pair of binoculars, held very carefully, we could observe the crescent shape of Venus at these times. These outings generated a lifetime interest in the heavens for me and my two brothers. My older brother, Gene, became an assistant astronomer for the University of California at Lick Observatory on Mt. Hamilton. While there he

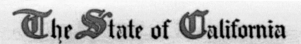

The State of California

Awards this Life Diploma to M. Esther Harlan

It authorizes the holder to teach in any Elementary School in the State. It shall remain valid during the life of the holder unless sooner revoked.

By order of the State Board of Education, at Sacramento, California, this first day of November, 1931, and attested by

Gordon Gray
Vice President State Board of Education

Superintendent of Public Instruction
and ex officio Secretary State Board of Education

LIFE DIPLOMA ISSUED TO M. ESTHER HARLAN

On November 1, 1931

Esther was granted this Life Diploma to teach in any public elementary school in the State of California. It was awarded by the State Board of Education after she had proven herself to be worthy of this lifetime license to teach.

discovered a long period comet (Comet Harlan 1976g), which was named after him.

Our teacher, Esther Harlan, would take us on nature hikes to observe the animals, birds, insects, reptiles, wild flowers, trees, grasses and even Indian relics. We were instructed to outline animal tracks for comparison to printed outlines of same in reference books at school.

We, students, were instructed to select specimens of plants and flowers native to the region and bring small samples to class for use in spatter printing of their shapes on paper. From these spatter prints we made a scrapbook of most of the native plants of the area. Esther instructed us to use four different types of spatter printing. Some of the samples were spatter printed on white paper with regular blue ink for spattering. We then colored in the leaves and flowers with colored pencils. In a second method a green paper was used and white paint was used for spatter, thereby forming the shape of the leaves on the green background paper. These and other samples were then framed on a background of colored paper sheets to form the scrapbook. These experiences allowed us to become familiar with all of the species of plants, to learn their names and to learn the spelling of the various names.

Honey bees, yellow jackets and bumble bees offered close-up inspection as they worked in gathering nectar from the flowers. At some distance we also saw how the honey bees carried nectar and pollen back to their hives for processing into bee bread, bee's wax and honey. My father maintained a number of bee hives on our property, which produced a quantity of honey each year. We watched closely as the yellow jackets manufactured paper from waste wood and saliva to enlarge their paper nests. We also observed them cutting off little cubes of red meat from venison, beef, or even cooked meat from our lunch sandwiches, and carrying it to their nests. We observed the various kinds of birds and their nests if possible. We were warned of the poisonous snakes and how to identify them.

The sites of the old Indian encampments were quite visible because of the dark soil, the sea shell residue, the abandoned stone tools, mortars, pestles, arrow heads

REDWOOD BRANCH SCHOOL STUDENTS
OF THE 1936-1937 SCHOOL YEAR

*BACK ROW left to right: Evelyn May Delvey, David Ernest Delvey and Edward
Harlan Kiplinger
FRONT ROW left to right: Donald Alwin Harlan, Stanley Vernon Harlan, and
Floyd Maynard Delvey*

*My father was just finishing up the school as we entered in the fall of 1936. It was
a great improvement over the cramped quarters that my mother taught school in at
our old house for a number of previous years. A receipt shows my father
purchased 705 feet of 1 inch and 40 feet of ¾ inch water pipe on August 1, 1936
for the school project. A ditch was dug and the one-inch pipe was installed from
the spring to the school and connected to the school plumbing fixtures by the time
school started in late August. It was our first experience with a drinking fountain
seen on the right.*

California Poppy

SPATTER PRINT OF CALIFORNIA POPPY
MADE BY REDWOOD SCHOOL STUDENTS

Redwood

SPATTER PRINT OF A REDWOOD LEAF BRANCH
MADE BY REDWOOD SCHOOL STUDENTS

and flint chips. These sites were so common on our ranch that we did not fully understand their importance to the history of the area. At the time I attended school there were still a few full-blooded native Indians living within a few miles. They had become quite well adjusted to "American" ways, and we were taught to have the greatest respect for them. One of these individuals, Antonio (Tony) Fontes, an outstanding vaquero, lived as a caretaker on a neighboring ranch and frequently helped my father with cattle round ups. His parents and brothers and sisters grew up on the coast near the headwaters of Mill Creek.

My mother took great interest in the happenings of the time. The Byrd expedition to the South Pole piqued her interest, and she faithfully listened to the daily broadcasts made from Antarctica. She then relayed the information to her students.

The U. S. Naval dirigible, The Macon, went down off Point Sur on the evening of February 12th, 1935. We, as students at Redwood School, were quite familiar with its passing by, quite frequently, on its regular trips from its homeport of Sunnyvale to Los Angeles and San Diego. On this fateful day, I remember seeing it pass a few miles off shore, between towering clouds and facing a strong northwest wind, as it had done on other occasions. Less than a half hour later that evening my mother received the news on the radio that it had gone down. She made an educational lesson for us the next day in class about the Macon and other dirigibles. I remember that she had received a sample of the Macon's "skin" when it was first built, which she used as a bookmark for many years. The navy also made an extreme effort to locate the two crew members who were lost in the crash. It seemed as though the whole Pacific fleet took part. There were all kinds of warships within the area. A few of them anchored no more than a couple of miles off our coast.

The reconstruction and refitting of Old Ironsides was brought to our attention, and all of us contributed a small sum toward its completion. Records indicate that it cost $987,000 between 1925 and 1931 for the rebuilding efforts. Of that figure school children contributed $148,000. In late September 1933, we observed the passing of Old Ironsides on the Big Sur coast as it passed in front of our ranch. Though it was capable of flying all 42,700 square feet of sail, it was shepherded (towed) by the USS Grebe, a minesweeper, and the USS Bushnell, a submarine tender. It toured a number of California cities on a goodwill tour and more than 2,000,000 California residents observed it as well.

The opening of the highway work road allowed Mr. Eckman from the Monterey County Office of Education to come 3 or 4 times a year with his movie projector, and he showed us interesting educational films on agriculture in the Salinas and San Joaquin valleys. He had a special truck with a bank of rechargeable batteries that he used for electricity to run the projector. He brought prepared lessons to us for later study, then, we were given tests, also prepared by Mr. Eckman, on the subject matter.

We also were visited by the County School's nurse, Mae Slater, who checked our vitals and gave us educational tips on good health. County Schools supervisor, Elmarie Dyke, also came and checked our curriculum to make sure we were being taught the right things.

The war years of 1941 through 1945 brought about many changes on the Big Sur coast. Highway travel dropped off to nearly zero because of the tight rationing of gasoline and tires. A number of businesses closed their doors for the duration. My father, because he was in the ranching business, had an adequate ration of gasoline, but tires were almost non-existent. We all became experts at getting another mile out of a given tire.

A detachment of United States Coastguardsmen came to our ranch in early 1942 and established a lookout station on a projecting piece of land on one of our fields. They commandeered the vacant housing from the Big Creek bridge construction crew at our Ranchito Creek. There were normally five members of the detachment (one officer and four seamen). They each stood four hour shifts at the lookout station 24 hours a day and seven days a week. They were to report any ships, aircraft or any other thing out of the ordinary. They also were responsible for their own food preparation and maintenance of the cabin barracks. This schedule became somewhat boring to many of them and contributed to their homesick feelings.

My mother took it upon herself to invite any, or all, of the coast guardsmen over to the house for a home cooked meal. Most of them, who were not on duty, obliged her offer and consequently created lifelong friendships.

My brother, Donald, and I also contributed to making the coast guardsmen's stay a little more bearable. We would frequently go on long hikes in the mountains which were of interest to some. We also went fishing or hunting frequently with others who seemed to appreciate the variation of their activities. We were both to

A LISTING OF MONTE

<u>SUMMARY OF MAJOR CROPS OF MONTEREY COUNTY FOR 1937</u>

Compiled by P. A. Kantor, County Agricultural Commissioner, A. A. Tavernetti, County Agenst, and R. Albaugh, Assistant County Agent. Estimates are used where records are not available. It is not presumed that these figures are accurate in all details.

Total acres in county	$ 2,131,200
Land in farms	1,205,065
Number of farms	2,100
Land in crops	220,000
Fallow or idle	50,525
Plowable pasture	85,000
Total land available for crops	355,245

<u>FIELD CROPS</u>

Crops	Crop acres	Estimated Farm Value
Artichokes	4,450	$ 1,112,500
Beans	55,637	3,121,089
Carrots	5,083	432,055
Cauliflower	1,065	82,986
Garlic	650	72,800
Lettuce	47,362	3,068,530
Onions	360	83,700
Peas	2,523	51,775
Potatoes	1,000	75,000
Spinach	350	3,500
Sugar Beets	10,177	1,401,828
Tomatoes (Shipping)	691	41,460
Tomatoes (Canning)	1,000	60,000
Misc Seed	5,873	392,700
Barley	42,500	1,050,000
Oats	1,000	16,200
Wheat	16,225	181,720
Hay (Grain)	20,000	200,000
Total	215,946	Total $ 11,447,843

ESTIMATED TOTAL FARM VALUE PRODUCED — $15,724,333

<u>FRUITS</u>

		Estimated Farm Value
Almonds	3,339 acres	173,400
Apples	1,933 "	96,320
Apricots	1,964 "	166,250
Cherries	85 "	40,000
Grapes	147 "	3,000
Peaches	135 "	9,000
Pears	1,004 "	195,000
Strawberries	150 "	72,000
Walnuts	242 "	35,000
Total	8,999	$ 789,970

<u>DAIRYING, LIVESTOCK, POULTRY, BEES</u>

	Number	
Beef cattle	45,250	944,960
Dairy cows	14,000 (butterfat)	1,650,600
	(beef & veal)	105,000
Sheep	20,650 (meat & wool)	173,460
Swine	23,480	270,000
Poultry	106,000 (eggs & meat)	346,000
Bees (colonies)	14,000 (honey)	36,500
	Total	$ 3,486,520

REY COUNTY FARM PRODUCTION IN 1937

This and the following two pages show an outline of the content of the agriculture program as it was taught in the county schools. It is interesting to note the values of roughly $16 million in 1937 have jumped to nearly 4 billion in 2008 (250 times as much).

AGRICULTURAL EDUCATION SERVICE

OF

OFFICE OF SUPERINTENDENT OF SCHOOLS OF MONTEREY COUNTY

Vol 15 - No. 1	1938-39
Jas. G. Force	O. L. Eckman
Superintendent of Schools	Director of Agricultural Instruction

AGRICULTURE

What is agriculture? This word comes from two Latin words, ager and cultura and means cultivation of the field. In modern times the word agriculture includes the production of domestic animals as well as plants. It is the fundamental occupation upon which all other occupations depend. We could get along without everything but food and clothing. There was a time, thousands of years ago, when our ancestors did not cultivate the field. By a slow process, they developed from savages to civilized beings. This development took place during four stages:

1. They lived in caves and secured their food by going out and hunting for it. At first they hunted fruit, nuts and roots.

2. Then they became braver and fished and hunted animals. Primitive man did not have fine rifles or revolvers with which to shoot his prey, he did not even have a bow and arrow. What he used seems very crude to us today, it was a stone ax without even a handle. Some very interesting things have been discovered in pre-historic caves which throw some light on the manner in which our ancestors lived. In one cave was found the skeleton of a very large cave bear. In his skull was embedded a crude stone ax. The bone had healed around the ax, leaving part of it exposed, which indicates that the bear had not been killed with the ax, but lived for some time after this hunt, and probably died from old age. We do not know what became of the man who wielded the ax, since the ax had no handle, the man who fought the bear must have done so at close range, and the bear may have killed him. As primitive man developed in intelligence, he developed his weapons and later he used a kind of bow and arrow. He also made drawings on the walls and ceilings of caves which show what wild animals, now extinct, looked like.

Man has made his greatest advance since he left the cave dwellings.

3. For a long time he was a shepherd and had flocks of sheep and herds of cattle. This made necessary the moving from place to place to find the best pasture. We therefore say that man was a "nomad" during his third stage of development. There are still many nomadic peoples, especially in Asia.

4. Finally he settled down to cultivate the fields, and lived in rude houses. When man had become quite civilized, he left records of his deeds and modes of living. We have learned much of early civilized man from the tombs of Egypt. It was the custom in Egypt 4000 years ago for a man to have inscribed (in Hieroglyphics, that is, picture writing) on his tomb how many sheep, goats, cattle and donkeys he owned. We also learn from these hieroglyphics something of the agricultural practices of early times. One picture shows a cattle round-up, the cattle and attendants passing by the reviewing stand of the owner. In another picture is shown a crude wooden plow to which two cattle are hitched. Such a plow only scratched the surface and did not turn over a furrow as do our modern plows.

So long as man had to spend most of his time hunting for food, he could

For the Year

1938 - 39

1. History of Agriculture

2. Agricultural Inventions & Machinery

3. Wheat

4. Corn

5. Beans

6. Cotton

7. Alfalfa

    Examination

8. Rubber

9. Potatoes

10. Lettuce

11. Sugar Beets

12. Domestic Animals

13. Breeds of Live Stock

14. Some principles of feeding and breeding animals

    Examination

15. Cattle

16-17-18. The Dairy Industry

19. The Horse

20. Diseases of Animals

21. Seeds

    Examination

22. Gardening

23. Principles of Forestry

24. Trees

25. Weeds

26. Insects

27. Birds

28. Camping

    Examination

be in the service soon thereafter, and it was of value to us to see the service man's life from both viewpoints.

In the early 1940's, The Moores had moved away and sold the property around our ranch to John Nesbitt of the popular radio program, "The Passing Parade," and later master of ceremonies of the "Telephone Hour" on television. My father no longer had to butcher beef for the Circle M Ranch as he had done for many years. He was able to maintain his grazing privileges on the ranch as he had done before with an acceptable agreement with Mr. Nesbitt.

During the war years of 1941 to 1945, my father reached maximum production of beef from his cattle operation. He sold his wiener calves at approximately six months of age to Salinas Dressed Beef Company in Watsonville and later Salinas, owned by the Errington family. They, in turn, had contracts with the Federal Government to supply this high-quality beef to the armed forces. My father did quite well financially under this arrangement.

He also increased the number of cows that he milked at the ranch each morning and evening during the winter and spring months. At one time, I remember the two of us milking thirty-two cows by hand each morning and evening. We did this chore before school in the morning and again in the evening hours just at dusk. My father then separated the cream from the milk on a hand operated milk separator. He sometimes spent as much as two hours after we went to school and again in the late evening after dinner just on separating the cream from the milk and then washing utensils afterward.

The cream was in great demand and was transported from the ranch to the creamery in five-gallon milk cans by the mail delivery man who came down the coast on Mondays, Wednesdays and Fridays from Monterey. Cream and butter were rationed at that time and my father received a premium price for his product. This was a lot of hard work over many hours each day, but it paid quite well. It was the first time that my father was able to afford major improvements on the ranch.

Redwood Branch School, due to declining enrollment, was closed the year I graduated in 1941. My mother did continue on a special contract, thru June of 1942, teaching (tutoring) just two students that year.

A VIEW OF THE COASTGUARD LOOKOUT SITUATED ON OUR PROPERTY DURING WORLD WAR II YEARS

Seaman Waldo Baker serving a four-hour shift at the facility. He, along with three other seamen and a warrant officer, made up the detachment of 5 service men who manned the lookout 24 hours a day and 7 days a week.

Near the end of World War II, my mother and father were asked by Mr. Nesbitt to move onto the Circle M Ranch, where my mother became their official cook. In this capacity she was able to concentrate on preparing meals without the restrictions of time or the concerns of clean-up afterward. She always had loved to cook and this gave her an opportunity to try recipes that had not been possible before. She also did some tutoring for the three Steck girls (Mr. Steck was a ghost writer for John Nesbitt's "Passing Parade" and acted as foreman for Mr. Nesbitt in the early days of the Nesbitt ownership) and young Michael Nesbitt.

My father continued with his ranching chores and also took on a number of special projects that Mr. Nesbitt requested of him. These projects included production of dairy products for use on the ranch in facilities previously used by Gus Carlson, the dairyman employed by the Moore ownership and kept on as overseer during the change of ownerships. Water development, construction of ranch roads, maintaining the local gardens and orchards, and even the excavation of a swimming pool were a few more projects that my father took on in the late 1940's for Mr. Nesbitt.

Gene Harlan, my oldest brother, used Mr. Nesbitt's TD14 bulldozer to construct the "new" road from the highway up to the Circle M Ranch during this period of time also.

Radio was a natural for Mr. Nesbitt and the "Passing Parade" proved to be very successful for him. He had started in the mid 1930s doing short subjects within other programs such as, "The Treasury Hour", "Fibber McGee and Molly" and the "Johnson's Wax Program". He was so well liked that he was given a full hour show which he produced and narrated himself with quite a large staff of researchers and other support personnel.

The advent of television in the late 1940s brought a number of challenges to Mr. Nesbitt. He was no longer a young man with the polish that the cameras required, though he did continue to have the utmost command of the English language. His insecurity in front of the cameras brought about excessive use of alcohol and the consequent loss of his marriage to his wife, Bea, and the loss of his job with MGM. He and Bea had one son, Michael, who my mother helped tutor for a period of time.

Mr. Nesbitt remarried soon after his divorce, and he moved to a home in the Carmel Highlands. He and his new wife, Priscilla, had two more children, Penny and Brian. Mr. Nesbitt's health deteriorated further, and he died at 49 years of age in August of 1960. The loss of income required giving up the ranch he so dearly loved.

The Circle "M" Ranch was put into the hands of a group of attorneys who sold the south third (which contained all of the ranch buildings) to Bill Earl and John Smart. The middle section was sold to a Mr. Potter and managed by Babe Bullard. The north section was held for a period of time by the group of attorneys and a Dr. Stotler. The lawyers and Dr. Stotler each staked out a few acres in Big Creek and areas nearby for their own use and a similar parcel was kept by Mr. Nesbitt's new wife, Pricilla. The area surrounding these parcels was later sold to the University of California for research purposes.

Mr. Packard, of Hewlett/Packard, purchased the central portion of the ranch which had been owned by Mr. Potter. He also purchased part of the lands held by Bill Earl and John Smart, except for section 9 and parts of section 16 which had previously been sold to the Camaldolese Hermitage. An additional parcel of 483.24 acres, previously owned by Marion Harlan, in the headwaters of Vicente Creek was also purchased by Mr. Packard.

My mother and father moved back to their own ranch in mid-1948, where my father started to build a very sturdy home on a site in Section 18 that he had chosen years before. A water system was already established and the ground had been cleared and leveled by a bulldozer in the 1930s. He put in a massive rock wall on the lower side of the house to form a level garden area for my mother. The foundation for the house and the rock wall consumed many cubic yards of concrete. Most of the sand and gravel was mixed on site after it had been acquired from a large beach in section 36. He purchased a small cement mixer powered by a Briggs and Stratton engine which; through the conscientious lubrication, cleaning and care of my brother, Donald; faithfully held up throughout the construction and is still used for smaller jobs today.

As time passed and more modern methods became available, my father purchased a Dodge 1 ½ ton stake truck on March 3, of 1939, which he used for hauling loose hay from the fields to the storage barn. He, along with Donald and Gene's help, built a cattle rack for it out of vertical steel "U" members from the stake pockets and then bolting 1" x 12" redwood boards to the vertical members. A loading chute was built onto a holding corral in the creek bottom just above the highway at the turn of the old work road. This made it possible for my father to load his fattened steers and haul them to market as far away as South San Francisco where the prices were two or three cents per pound higher than dealing with the local buyers.

His next purchase was a narrow-gauge Caterpillar "30" track laying tractor and a disc plow which he used in place of the horse team and the sidehill plow. The horses were allowed retirement on the ranch and died natural deaths many years later. The Caterpillar "30" had a straight (non-angled) bulldozer blade which could be used for general clearing of roads and brush on nearly level ground. It proved to be a learning tool for all of us in operating such equipment. It was quite dangerous in road building because the load of dirt and rocks in front of the blade could not be discharged off the edge easily. These characteristics demonstrated inadequacy for making new roads on the ranch as my father had hoped it might, however. The tractor was sold to the Fife family who used it at their saw mill in Big Creek to push logs onto the mill carriage in preparation to mill them into lumber.

The tractor was replaced, after World War Two, as soon as military construction was converted to civilian output, with a wide gauge International diesel TD 9. The TD 9 had a fully adjustable blade to angle in either direction or to use in the straight blade configuration. It proved to be very valuable in the construction of our ranch roads. All three of us boys and my father became quite proficient in its operation. My brother, Gene, and I used it for a year (1948-1949) in our venture of falling, bucking, loading and hauling ponderosa pine from the Gamboa area of the ranch to the mill in Big Creek. We built the road from the mill site to the ridge above the Marble Place (now Whale Point) so we could truck the log sections to the mill. Gene and my father had built the rest of the road on that section of the ranch earlier while I was in the military service. The TD9 was still in use on the ranch in 2007 (more than 60 years after it was manufactured).

The Dodge truck was replaced with a new 2 ½ ton chassis bed GMC in February 1950. As before, Donald and my father constructed a steel beam supported flat bed of 2-inch-thick redwood planks on this chassis. They also built a cattle rack of steel and redwood lumber to complete the project. This truck was purchased with the intent of hauling larger loads of cattle and hay. The expansion of the cattle raising activity required the hauling of many loads of cattle to market each year. Additional corrals with loading chutes were built at a number of locations on the ranch as well. The truck was also used to haul the TD 9 to various parts of the ranch and even to neighboring ranches to do work for hire. This truck was still being used on the ranch until 2007 (over 57 years after it was manufactured).

In 1953, during and after the construction period of the new ranch house my father purchased a used 1942 International dump truck. A large amount of excavation

STATE TEACHERS' RETIREMENT SYSTEM
1408 Jay Street
Sacramento 14, California

Mrs. M. Esther Harlan   September 1, 1954
Big Sur
California

Dear Mrs. Harlan:

Enclosed is a copy of a self-explanatory letter sent today to the County Superintendent
of the County in which you were employed.

The following information is furnished about your Retirement System status, the effective
date of your retirement being   August 1 , 19 54 :

1. Amount of your monthly retirement allowance
    a. Permanent Fund retirement salary $ 28.75
    b. Retirement Annuity Fund Annuity $ 50.31
    c. Annuity Deposit Fund Annuity $ -- --
    d. Total monthly allowance subject to deductions in (7), if any $ 79.06

2. Permanent Fund contributions required
    e. $12.00 per year for 10¼ years prior to July 1, 1935 $ 123.00
    f. $24.00 per year for   7 years from July 1,1935 to June 30,1944 $ 168.00
    g. $60.00 per year for   0 years from July 1, 1944 $ -- --
    h. Total contributions required $ 291.00

3. Permanent Fund contributions standing to your credit
    at the time of retirement $ 281.75

4. Balance of Permanent Fund contributions due   (2) - (3) $ 9.25

5. Contributions included in (4) which would have been paid
    during the period you were exempt, were excluded because of
    other System membership, or were teaching outside California $

6. Interest at 5% per annum, not compounded, on contributions in
    (5) from July 1st next following the school year in which the
    amounts were due, to the date of retirement, time during which
    you were under retirement, if previously retired, being excluded $

7. Total amount due on account of Permanent Fund contributions in
    arrears   (4) + (6) $ 9.25

8. Retirement Annuity Fund contributions, excluding interest,
    standing to your credit at the time of retirement $

9. Annuity Deposit Fund contributions, excluding interest,
    standing to your credit at the time of retirement $

10. Total contributions made during active service and standing
    to your credit at retirement   (3) + (8) + (9) $ 281.75

The amount due in item (7) will be deducted from your monthly allowance at the rate of
$ 12.00 per month until the total is paid. The deduction from your first retirement
allowance warrant (regardless of whether the warrant is for one or a fraction of one
month, or possibly for more than one month because of time required to complete your
records) will be either the rate per month multiplied by the months and fraction thereof
covered, or the entire amount in (7), whichever is smaller.

Total contributions credited to you at retirement, are shown in item (10) for federal and
state income tax purposes. The Retirement Office does not give advice about tax matters.
If you need such advice, you should take this letter to your tax advisor or to representatives of the Federal and State Income Tax Bureaus.

CALIFORNIA STATE TEACXHER'S RETIREMENT SYSTEM
CALCULATION SHEET FOR ESTHER HARLAN'S RETIREMENT

was necessary just above the house and the dump truck, in combination with the John Deere loader, proved a very efficient way to remove and haul away the material to a dumping site. My brother, Gene, had come back to the ranch for an extended stay to help my father with his projects. Gene did most of the excavation work mentioned here. Both the Dodge truck and the International truck died a slow death on the ranch and were eventually sold as scrap metal.

The TD9 proved to be a little large for haying operations so my father also purchased a John Deere model 4401 CD (diesel) 2 cylinder track laying tractor to handle the lighter chores on the ranch. It was equipped with a small loader bucket which my brother, Donald, modified to handle a buck rake for loading loose hay onto the truck. All of these improvements allowed my father to raise oat hay on additional acreage on section 36 field between Vicente Creek and Big Creek. Cutting, raking, baling and hauling hay was a regular summer activity for me, my brother, Donald, and my father. Gene had moved away from the ranch in the early 1940s and was employed by war production companies as a machinist.

After the three of us boys left the ranch for our other lifetime endeavors, my father also bought an Oliver, Model G No. 8 Baler which could be pulled behind the tractor and pick up the hay from the field directly out of the windrows, thereby eliminating the arduous task of hand shocking.

The Dodge truck was replaced with a new 2 ½ ton chassis bed GMC in February 1950. As before, Donald and my father constructed a steel beam supported flat bed of 2-inch-thick redwood planks on this chassis. They also built a cattle rack of steel and redwood lumber to complete the project. This truck was purchased with the intent of hauling larger loads of cattle and hay. The expansion of the cattle raising activity required the hauling of many loads of cattle to market each year. Additional corrals with loading chutes were built at a number of locations on the ranch as well. The truck was also used to haul the TD 9 to various parts of the ranch and even to neighboring ranches to do work for hire. This truck was still being used on the ranch until 2007 (over 57 years after it was manufactured).

In 1953, during and after the construction period of the new ranch house my father purchased a used 1942 International dump truck. A large amount of excavation was necessary just above the house and the dump truck, in combination with the John Deere loader, proved a very efficient way to remove and haul away the material to a dumping site. My brother, Gene, had come back to the ranch for an extended stay to help my father with his projects. Gene did most of the excavation

DISK PLOW USED BY THE HARLANS FROM THE 1940's ON

George Harlan purchased this disk plow in the 1940's and it was used until the ranch was sold in 2007. A selected field was plowed and sown with red oat seed. Upon maturity for hay the oats were cut, raked, cured, shocked or baled, then hauled to the barn for winter feeding of stock.

The disk was also effective to kill small brush plants that would overtake the grassy fields if unattended. The grass was allowed to mature and develop seed and feed for the animals. In the late summer the disk was then used to turn the dry grass and young brush invaders over to stifle the growth of the brush. The grass seed mixed with the plowed soil and sprouted after fall rains replenishing the grass crop for the following year. This technique proved very successful on areas that were not to steep.

THE HARLAN'S INTERNATIONAL TD9 BULLDOZER

This machine was purchased by George Harlan in 1947 soon after International Harvester converted from World War II production to civilian production. It proved to be a tremendous boon to our ranching industry. It could be used to plow the fields for the raising of hay and all of the other tasks related to cutting, raking, and bailing of hay for use on the ranch. It was used for making many of the ranch roads which allowed my father to transport stock and feed to all parts of the four ranges that he maintained for grazing of his extensive cattle herd. It was used by Gene and Stanley in 1948 and 1949 to haul and load mill logs to the saw mill in Big Creek. It was used for hire by Donald to build roads and perform other major tasks for neighboring ranches and mining interests. All of us learned to become quite proficient in its use at the ranch. Donald and Gene did major repairs and rebuilding of the machine itself over the years. Engine overhauls, track replacement, bull gear replacement were a few examples.

work mentioned here. Both the Dodge truck and the International truck died a slow death on the ranch and were eventually sold as scrap metal.

The TD9 proved to be a little large for haying operations so my father also purchased a John Deere model 4401 CD (diesel) 2-cylinder track laying tractor to handle the lighter chores on the ranch. It was equipped with a small loader bucket which my brother, Donald, modified to handle a buck rake for loading loose hay onto the truck. All of these improvements allowed my father to raise oat hay on additional acreage on section 36 field between Vicente Creek and Big Creek. Cutting, raking, baling and hauling hay was a regular summer activity for me, my brother, Donald, and my father. Gene had moved away from the ranch in the early 1940s and was employed by war production companies as a machinist.

After the three of us boys left the ranch for our other lifetime endeavors, my father also bought an Oliver, Model G No. 8 Baler which could be pulled behind the tractor and pick up the hay from the field directly out of the windrows, thereby eliminating the arduous task of hand shocking.

My mother enjoyed her new home with many conveniences that she had not had in any of her previous locations. Exceptions were highline power and public telephone service. She purchased a large propane operated Servel refrigerator, a new propane operated gas range, kitchen cabinets, a large stainless-steel kitchen sink and other conveniences throughout the house. She enjoyed the advent of television and soon purchased a large console television which she watched in the evenings. Reception there was very poor because the location was 88 miles from the transmitter in San Luis Obispo or even farther to the transmitter in Santa Barbara. Only two stations were at all possible, and it was only through the extended efforts of my brother, Donald, who upgraded the T V antennas frequently, that reception came through at all. It was necessary to operate a 2 ½ KW electric generator at times when she watched television or did washing or ironing and, of course, electric lighting in the house.

My Mom was a very social person, and she joined a number of social organizations there on the Big Sur coast. She hosted various groups at her house throughout the 1950s and early 1960s. She continued to cook and garden in a very diligent manner. She faithfully corresponded with her daughter in law, Irene, (my wife) every week and also maintained contact with many of her friends and acquaintances. She even continued correspondence with some of the U S Coast Guardsmen who had been stationed on our ranch from 1942 through 1945. She always greeted visitors with a hearty meal and a promise of overnight lodging if

OWNERSHIP AND THE LAST REGISTRATION FOR MY FATHER'S
1935 DODGE STAKE BED TRUCK

This truck, purchased on March 10, 1939, allowed my father to haul his hay from the fields to the barns in an efficient manner. It also allowed him to haul his cattle to market where a better price was offered for his beef.

COPY OF OWNERSHIP AND REGISTRATION FOR MY FATHER'S
1942 INTERNATIONAL DUMP TRUCK

This truck was used by my father to haul excavated dirt from his house building project and also for hauling sand and gravel for concrete construction on many other projects.

Farmers Insurance Exchange

SUPERSEDING

DECLARATIONS

Item 1. Name of Insured **GEORGE A. HARLAN**
Address **BIG SUR**
CALIFORNIA

Policy No. **74684**

District Agent
51 87 WARD & SON
01
Local Agent

The named insured is **INDIVIDUAL** Occupation of the named insured is **RANCHER**

Item 2. Policy Period: From time applied for on 12:01 A. M. Standard Time, at the address of the named insured as stated herein and additional terms of six calendar months each for which the required premium is paid. **MAY 8, 1950** to **JULY 1, 1950**

Item 3. The insurance afforded is only with respect to such and so many of the following coverages as are indicated by specific Premium Deposit charge or charges. The limit of the Exchange's liability against each such coverage shall be as stated herein, subject to all of the terms of this policy having reference thereto:

COVERAGES	Limits of Liability		Premium Deposit	Membership Fee
A—Bodily Injury Liability	$ 15,000 each person	$30,000 each accident	12.52	CR
B—Property Damage Liability	$ 5,000 each accident			
C & D—Fire, Lightning & Transportation and Theft	Actual Cash Value		5.40	CR
E—Comprehensive (Including Fire & Theft)	Actual Cash Value			
F—Collision or Upset	Actual Cash Value Less			
		Deductible		
F—1 Towing and Road Service Expense	$ 10 each disablement			
G—Medical Payments	$ 250. each person		1.50	
Special charges as per endorsement attached				

Cash Credit $ Other Credit $ TOTAL   Cr.   Bal.

Description of the automobile and the facts respecting its purchase by named insured:

Year Model & Trade Name	Type of Body, (Truck Tonnage Trailer Length) Serial	Numbers	No. Cyls.	Model	Actual Cost Including Equipment	Date Purchased Month Day—Year	New or Used?
1950	G M C	2½ TON FLATBED A 270 762 686	6		3300.	2-50	NEW

Item 4. The purposes for which the automobile is to be used are: "Pleasure and Business" or "Farm Purposes" unless otherwise stated herein:

(a) The term "pleasure and business" is defined as personal, pleasure, family and business use. (b) The term "commercial" is defined as use principally in the business occupation of the named insured as stated in item 1, including occasional use for personal, pleasure, family and other business purposes. (c) The term "farm purposes" is defined as use principally on or about the named insured's farm premises in connection with the operation of the named insured's farm, and includes "pleasure and business" use. (d) Use of the automobile for the purposes stated includes the loading and unloading thereof.

Item 5. The automobile will be principally garaged in the above Town, County and State, unless otherwise stated herein.

Item 6. The automobile described is unencumbered except as herein stated: Amount $ Last Payment Due

Any loss under Coverages C, D, E and F is payable as interest may appear to the named insured and

(Name)

(Address)

Item 7. Except with respect to bailment lease, conditional sale, mortgage or other encumbrance, the named insured is the sole owner of the automobile except as herein stated.

Item 8. During the past year no insurer has cancelled any automobile insurance issued to the named insured except as herein stated.

Attached to and forming part of policy numbered above, issued by Farmers Insurance Exchange at

LOS ANGELES, CALIFORNIA, MAY 12, 1950--1GB
Place of Issuance   Date

FARMERS-INSURANCE EXCHANGE
Farmers Underwriters Association Atty. in fact.

Countersigned *L. R. Davidson*

By *T. E. Leavey*
President

ACT - M650 - 200M - 1-50 ⑦

**INSURANCE RECORD SHOWING DETAILS OF MY FATHER'S
OWNERSHIP OF HIS 2 ½ TON GMC TRUCK**

DONALD AND GEORGE HARLAN LOADING SHOCKS OF LOOSE HAY IN THE FIELD BELOW OUR OLD HOUSE

Early 1950's

Donald is using the John Deere loader to pick up whole shocks of hay with the buck rake attachment he made for the front of the loader. George is atop the load of hay spreading the new delivery, by hand with a pitchfork, to tie it in with the rest of the load. This process allowed two people to load the hay from the field to the truck. Previously, it required at least two people on the ground to lift the hay with pitchforks from the shocks to the top of the load.

Marion Harlan is helping with a pitchfork to clean up bits of loose hay still on the ground. Esther Harlan is looking on. Shorty and Butch are checking for mice.

PACIFIC GAS AND ELECTRIC COMPANY

OFFICES

Carmel
Dolores Street
L. G. Weer
Local Manager

Hollister
321 Fifth St.
Wayne Matthews
District Manager

King City
118 South Third St.
H. E. Laffingwell
District Manager

Monterey
485 Tyler St.
G. E. Cunningham
District Manager

Pacific Grove
602 Lighthouse Ave.
C. A. Hicks
Local Manager

Paso Robles
617 - 12th Street
J. W. Dunlap
Local Manager

San Luis Obispo
894 Monterey Street
M. A. Wood
District Manager

Santa Maria
206 West Main Street
L. C. Stone
District Manager

COAST VALLEYS DIVISION
161 Main Street
Salinas, California
T. E. Ward, Division Manager

In reply please refer to

April 24, 1956

TO THE RESIDENTS OF GORDA - LUCIA:

As you know, a survey of prospective electric customers was recently conducted from Dolan Creek to Lucia, at the request of Mrs. Lulu Harlan, and from Lucia to Gorda at the request of other interested parties.

Results of the Lucia survey are as follows:

Dolan Creek (Hudson Jr. Property) to Lucia including Circle M Ranch but not Big Creek:

8 lights	3200'	
4 refrig. or freezers	800'	
5 ranges	6500'	
6 water heaters	3600'	
8 KW heat	280'	
5 KW commercial lights	1000'	
Free footage	15380'	

Approximate lineal distance	48000'	
Free footage	15380'	
Excess footage	32620'	
	.60	
Cash advance required in accordance with Extension Rule #15	$19,572.00	

Distance - (via map and speedometer) 9.2 miles

With an approximately 3100' free footage allowance to 2 dwellings two miles up Big Creek, around $4,400 additional advance would be required to build this tap.

COST QUOTATION FROM PG&E FOR EXTENSION OF SERVICE
TO THE LUCIA AREA FROM DOLAN CANYON
April 24, 1956

ESTHER AND GEORGE HARLAN AT THEIR 50TH WEDDING
ANNIVERSARY AT THE BIG SUR GRANGE HALL

Oct. 29, 1966

Pioneers in the greatest sense, Esther and George weathered through 50 years of hard work, many successes, a few failures, and a myriad of changes around them. Through it all, they stuck together with determination to improve their life and that of their three sons. My mother passed away just two years after this picture was taken leaving a very lonely George. I don't think they would have done it any other way.

GEORGE AND ESTHER HARLAN GETTING READY TO CUT THEIR
GOLDEN WEDDING ANNIVERSARY CAKE

October 29, 1966

A group of very thoughtful and giving people came together to honor my parents on their 50th wedding anniversary. The effort was spearheaded by my two aunts, Ada and Marian Smith, but many other friends and neighbors from the Big Sur coast also took part. We shall always be thankful for their participation.

In that 50-year period my parents saw the mountain trails forgiven for a modern highway. They saw the horse and buggy given up for the automobile. They experienced the birth and growth of the radio, the television, the airplane, the helicopter and many other developments not foreseen when they married in 1916. My mother even achieved her right to vote.

ESTHER AND GEORGE HARLAN AT THE RANCH ON THEIR
50TH WEDDING ANNIVERSARY

October 29, 1966

Upon returning from their anniversary party at the Big Sur Grange this picture was taken in the late afternoon of George and Esther outside their home at Lopez Point. It was not often that George put on a suit and necktie, but this was one of those rare occasions.

Esther was experiencing problems with her eyes as a result of glaucoma for a number of years, but she continued to be very active. Just two years later she passed on with heart failure.

THREE SISTERS--ADA SMITH, ESTHER HARLAN AND MARIAN
SMITH BY ESTHER'S DEODAR CEDAR TREE AT THE RANCH

October 29, 1966

My mother and my two aunts were very close to one another. All three were teachers of the California Public School System. Ada taught at New Idra, Redwood and Pacific Grove Unified. Marian taught at Redwood, Pacific Valley, Del Monte and Pacific Grove Unified. Esther taught at Redwood and Redwood Branch. Ada and Marian never married and had no children.

there was a need. Her sisters, Ada and Marian, continued to visit during the summers and her sons and daughters in law, with their families were always welcome for extended stays.

During this period of time my mother and father took a number of summer automobile tours of the western states and Canada with Mom's two sisters. It was usually expected that Irene and I and our daughter, Carmen, stay at the ranch to milk the cows, feed the pigs and chickens and to carry out all of the other daily chores at the ranch.

My mother suffered from glaucoma and cholesterol problems later in life. She still tried to carry on as she had done for so many years, but it was no longer possible. She passed away in October of 1968, suffering from heart failure.

My father had to give up his lease on the south two thirds of the ranch in 1954, when the legal group handling Mr. Nesbitt's affairs sold that portion of the ranch to Bill Earl and John Smart. That necessitated building new fences surrounding our property. He maintained a lease of the property north of Big Creek for a number of years or until 1969. The sale of the Earl and Smart holdings to Mr. Packard allowed my father to again graze cattle on the area south of Vicente Creek which he continued until his death, due to a vehicle accident on his beloved ranch in 1985.

In the early 1980s my father was nearing 90 years of age and was unable to act quickly on lion kills. He lost 39 head of calves, from a herd size of 40 cows, over a three-year period to mountain lions alone. This represented a third of the potential production. A number of these predators were treed by the government trapper and the contents of the lion's stomachs, analyzed at the University of California at Davis, were confirmed to be that of Harlan beef.

After my father's death my brother, Don, and I tried to continue with the cattle raising business. Don lived at the ranch and I only helped on planned occasions. The mountain lion population literally exploded to numbers that were far in excess of available food supplies. We continued to loose calves and the deer population plummeted to near zero in just a few years. The lions even resorted to killing harbor seals that would rest and bear young on our beaches. Once numerous raccoons, opossums, ring tailed cats, bobcats, skunks, civet cats and foxes all became food for the lions. We even experienced loss of pet cats and dogs.

The starvation of the excess number of mountain lions and the potential of human attacks by them in the Lopez Point region is the final consequence of present-day game management. "Let nature take its course" is the slogan. ***What an unnecessarily cruel way to manage our forests, our stock and wildlife!***

MY MOM AND DAD
(HISTORICAL PICTURES)

Though I have placed a number of pictures along with my parent's story, I would still like to add a number of additional pictures with descriptive subtitles to help convey the lifestyle and circumstances of their stay at Lopez Point. Many of the early pictures were taken with a simple Kodak box camera in black and white. Few of them are of professional quality, but they still are able to convey many things about the ranch and the people who lived there.

Most of the later pictures were taken with more modern camera equipment. Originally clear and sharp these slides and pictures have faded their colors over the years and are not now of the best quality.

I am including them here so that more people may share in our family collections.

A REPRODUCION OF THE CATTLE BRAND OF GEORGE HARLAN

This brand was officially registered with the State of California on October 29, 1915, just one year, to the day, before his marriage to Esther. The official registry appears on page 119 of Volume B of "Brands" at the Monterey County Recorder's Office in Salinas, California. It was maintained by the family until 2007, when the ranch was sold.

SOW WITH PIGLETS ON THE GEORGE AND ESTHER HARLAN RANCH

Circa 1920's

My father raised pigs throughout his life as an adjunct to his cattle raising operation. In the early days it was planned for the sow to bear young in the early spring when there would be adequate green grass for her to eat in order for her to produce the milk for her litter. There was usually a surplus of milk products at this time of year as well, so she supplemented her diet with whey, sour milk, cottage cheese and buttermilk. In the summer she was allowed into the barley patch where she and her half-grown offspring took their fill of mature barley. In the early fall the pigs were reaching maturity and they were taken to the wooded canyons to feast on tanoak acorns and finally, as live oak acorns matured, the pigs ranged through the wooded sidehills where the live oak trees grew. In late October the fattened pigs were gathered from the various ranches and herded[3] as a massive group to market, in King City, over the narrow mountain trails.

---

[3] This was a seven-day ordeal when my father was young. A lead horseman (my grandfather) dribbled dry corn from his horse along the trail which favorite pigs eagerly followed. The rest of the pigs would follow those leaders with some prodding by a number of people and dogs. They moved slowly to prevent overheating and rested frequently. At predetermined locations where there were picket fence enclosures for spending the night.

ADA SMITH (ESTHER HARLAN'S SISTER) WITH PIGS
AT THE GEORGE AND ESTHER HARLAN RANCH CIRCA 1925

Esther's two sisters (Ada and Marian) and her mother (Lucy Smith) were frequent summer visitors to the George and Esther Harlan ranch. They helped Esther with the daily activities and also participated in many of the ranch experiences. Here, Ada is scratching the gentle pigs with a stick to their enjoyment.

CATCH OF TROUT FROM VICENTE CREEK
Circa 1930's

My mother, along with aunts Marian and Ada, made frequent trout fishing excursions in the summer months to Vicente Creek via horseback and the Coast Trail. Grass hoppers were caught along the way on the grassy ridges and used for bait. This string represents two limits of 25 trout—a good feast for the Harlan/Smith crowd.

Note the tiered logs in the background forming level flower gardens on the sloped ground below the Old Harlan House. My mother won recognition from a national magazine for the submission of her descriptive and photographic flower beds.

A GROUP OF HARLAN CATTLE IN OUR CORRAL AT SECTION 36
Circa 1939

This was one of our collection points for cattle on the range between Vicente Creek and Big Creek. This corral had a loading chute which allowed us to load or unload cattle from our truck. Another corral near Vicente Creek at Palos Quatros was used for branding and other rodeo operations but did not have access to a roadway. This range could support approximately 75 head of adult cattle. My father, Donnie Smith and Tony Fontes rode horse back on our roundups. Marion Harlan, my brothers, and I were usually on foot with our dogs to rustle the cattle out of the brushy areas and to head them off at known trail crossings. These roundups proved to be very stressful. I remember bleeding from the lungs from over exertion and sometimes tumbling down the steep hillsides head over heels because the feet could not keep up to the body speed in an effort to reach a trail crossing ahead of the wayward herd.

OUR THREE DOGS AT THE HARLAN RANCH
Circa 1929

Dixie on the left, Browny (a puppy) looking over fence, and Sport on the right. We usually had three dogs while we were growing up. They were mixed breeds and were able at many skills. They excelled at treeing wild animals and we were called upon many times to go dispatch their quarry. Coyotes would not tree, but they occasionally made a mistake and got cornered in a hollow tree or a rock cave. The coyotes would sometimes entice our dogs at night time to chase them a distance from the house, then gang up on the dogs and chase them back to the house for safety.

DONALD AND GENE HARLAN NEAR OUR OLD HOUSE
Circa 1927

My two brothers before I was born. Gene was already old enough to do many of the simpler chores around the ranch. Both of them are nearing a need for a haircut. My father cut our hair with a hand operated clipper. We did not look forward to the experience because there was always a certain amount of hair pulling that accompanied the clipping operation.

DONALD HARLAN AT THE BEACH NEAR THE MOUTH OF THE CREEK
Circa 1927

My mother went to the beach quite frequently to try her luck at fishing from the shore. She used abalone for bait and typically fished with a "poke" pole with a one-foot long piece of chalk line and a number 6-0 hook attached to the small end. The poke pole was simply inserted into a likely hole under a rock where a fish may be waiting for an easy meal. She also used a throw line consisting of a chalk line 25 or 30 feet long wrapped on a wooden shingle to prevent kinks. The throw line required a weight (rock) at the outer end to hold it in place in the moving currents of water. A similar hook and bait was used at its end. Fishing was good!

DONALD HARLAN RESTING NEAR THE SITE OF OUR NEW HOME
Circa 1950

All of us helped in building my father and mother's new home. Donald probably did the most since Gene and I were working in the timber in 1948 and 1949, and I, later, was in attendance at UCSB.

ESTHER HARLAN FRYING FISH AT THE BEACH
July 4, 1938

We always looked forward to the 4th of July because my aunts would usually bring fireworks and we would have a fishing party at the beach, then, set off fireworks after dark. We chose an area where there would be no fire danger.

MY MOTHER, ESTHER HARLAN, FEEDING A PET
BLUEJAY AT OUR OLD HOUSE
Summer, 1944

My mother loved to see the wild birds and animals in this coastal region of the Harlan Ranch. George had caught a young brush rabbit while cutting hay and had given it to my aunt Marian to keep as a pet. The cage in the background was for that purpose. My uncle Fred had given the blue jay to Esther, but it was never penned up. My father had found some young mountain quail which we kept in a large wired enclosure behind the Old House. These quail prospered and multiplied there for many years.

DONALD HARLAN IN THE SERVICE OF OUR COUNTRY
Circa 1946

Donald took his military training at Camp Hunter Liggett in California. From there he was assigned to the Aleutian Islands at Adak where he served most of his duty. He was discharged in October of 1946, at Camp Beal, California, just a few days after Stanley's entry into the armed services.

ESTHER HARLAN ON TRIXIE HEADED FOR A DAY OF TEACHING
AT REDWOOD SCHOOL
Circa 1928

Sport, our family dog, Gene, Stanley, Esther and Donald are shown. Donald and I were not yet of school age. My mother made this trip many times while she was teaching at Redwood School. The school house was located about ½ mile beyond the ridge top over Esther's head.

GENE AND DONALD NEAR THE OLD HOUSE
Easter 1928

My mother and her two sisters usually made something special at Easter time. They would make up baskets of colored eggs and candy, then, hide them in an area near the house where we were to find them.

GENE NEAR OUR BACK-YARD GATE WITH HIS FIRST BUCK
Circa 1930's

All of us became good marksmen with a rifle. Each of us hunted deer in season as soon as we were big enough to do the dressing of the carcass. We supplemented our diet on these occasions with venison. We could not afford to kill our pigs or beef since they were our cash crop. We could only keep the meat for a few days because we had no refrigeration. We sometimes dried the meat for jerky but most commonly my mother canned the meat in quart jars with the aid of a pressure cooker.

She also canned mincemeat for use later in mincemeat pies. As I prefaced earlier in this tribute, I don't see how she could have found the time or energy to do all of these things. Her pie crusts were made from scratch and always were of the utmost quality. We were weaned on puddings, pies and cakes!

GENE AND MY MOTHER, ESTHER, WITH HARLAN PIGS IN FIELD
NEAR "COON" DITCH
Circa 1926

Pig raising was always a part of my father's ranching. He got his start from his father who encouraged his boys to clear land, plant barley and raise a few litters of pigs to get their start in life. It proved to be advantageous to his children as well as to the clearing of his ranch of brush.

Pigs were marketed in either King City or Monterey in the fall after the acorn crops were finished. Driving (coaxing) the pigs over nearly 50 miles of trail to King City proved to be quite arduous and took 5 days to accomplish. An alternative was to load the mature pigs on a fishing launch at a homemade cable landing and take them to Monterey by boat. The pigs typically got seasick and lost considerable weight before they were sold at the railroad stock yards near the Del Monte Hotel (now the Naval Postgraduate School). The pigs were unceremoniously pushed off the boat near the beach in Monterey and they swam to shore, then, gathered in a group on the beach totally bewildered and lost. From there they were herded to the stockyard corrals.

GENE WITH A HOMEMADE BOW AND ARROW NEAR REDWOOD
SCHOOL

March 1928

My aunt Marian was teaching Redwood School this year and she had only a few students. I think she was helping Gene act out to be an "Indian hunter". My mother had recently given birth to me and Marian was hired by the District to fill in until Esther was again able to teach. It was Marian's first assignment at teaching and she normally carried a Kodak Box camera. It is for this reason that we were left with so many historical pictures of the 1928-1929 period.

GENE HARLAN ON HIS GRADUATION FROM HIGH SCHOOL

June 1938

Gene completed his high school education at Monterey High School from 1934-1938. He stayed with his grandmother, Lucy, and his aunts Ada and Marian Smith who were teaching and living on the peninsula at that time. He made an effort to get back to the ranch on weekends and holidays so he could help my father with all of the ranching chores.

GEORGE HARLAN DISCUSSING HIS HIGHWAY CONSTRUCTION
INCONVENIENCES WITH ONE OF THE STATE ENGINEERS
Circa 1934

When the highway was cut through our property in 1933, there were certain agreements made by the State to compensate my father and mother for loss of buildings, loss of pasture land, need for fencing, removal of rocks from fields and a number of other disruptions. My parents had donated the right of way to the State for the highway and were not asking for any financial payment, but these other agreements raised some conflict here and there. Some of the problems were worked out by discussions such as this.

A GROUP OF HORSES ON THE OPEN RANGE

August 1931

Having extra horses and mules in the early days was a necessity for the ranchers. The narrow mountain trails were our "highways" and the horse was our mode of transportation. This scene was on the Coast Trail just northwest of the Vicente Creek crossing. Ada Smith is on the near horse.

VIEW OF THE GRANARY AND BARN FROM THE CORNER OF THE
GEORGE AND ESTHER HARLAN'S OLD HOUSE

February 1950

*Lopez Rock can be seen near right corner of the granary roof with highway guard
rail showing just below that. The hay barn was below the highway and at the time
of this photograph was still being used to store hay. Note the split redwood board
construction of the siding on the house.*

GEORGE HARLAN AND HIS TEAM OF HORSES PULLING THE WAGON
THROUGH A RECENTLY PLANTED POTATO PATCH ON THE BIG FLAT

July 1930

My father sometimes put in a few acres of corn and potatoes in one of the fields for later use as pig feed and chicken feed. It is hard to tell what is being hauled across the field in this picture. I remember hoeing the weeds from the corn and potato fields by hand when the crops were about this tall. It seemed as though we would "never" finish.

**A FAMILY GROUP TRAVELING THE COAST TRAIL AT THE BLUE SLIDE
JUST NORTH OF LIME KILN CREEK**
Circa 1930

This is a scene of the way we traveled from one place to another before the highway was constructed. The Coast Trail paralleled the ocean for the most part and averaged an elevation of 600 feet. The trail passed through most of the coastal ranches and, off course, many gates along the way. A cardinal sin was to leave a gate open after passing through it.

LUCY SMITH, OUR GRANDMOTHER, WITH STANLEY AND DONALD
ABOVE THE HARLAN RANCH HOUSE
Circa 1929

Lucy Smith always came to the ranch with Ada and Marian from Monterey during the summer months to visit the Harlan family. She loved to sit on the front porch and watch the large ships pass by. In those days the shipping along the west coast was quite varied and the lumber schooners supplying the Los Angeles area from the northwest passed close to shore on their northerly trip. They were usually empty and rode high on the water. Northwest winds were common and they hugged the shore to reduce fuel use. Many times the propellers would not be totally submerged and would make very load plop, plop, plop noises.

MARIAN SMITH HOLDING TWO SQUEALING PIGS JUST BELOW OUR
OLD GRANARY AT THE HARLAN RANCH

July 1927

*Both of my aunts seemed to enjoy the variety of experiences at the ranch. They
helped with the housework for my mother and volunteered for many of the daily
tasks with the pigs, the chickens, the calves, cutting wood, gardening, etc. They
also loved to go to the beach on abalone gathering or fishing trips and to the
creeks for trout fishing. They seemed to make all of the jobs entertaining to all.*

ADA SMITH ON BUCKSKIN, ESTHER HARLAN ON BABE AND GENE
HARLAN AND DOGS FOLLOWING UP THE REAR

June 1930

A note on the original picture indicates they were off on a wild strawberry picking excursion on the Harlan ranch. When I was small we did this quite frequently in the early summer months when the wild strawberries were ripening. There were certain locations on the ranch where the strawberries flourished. We would pick them into a glass canning jar, and we typically were able to get nearly a quart of berries on an outing.

My mother, a great cook, would mix them in with whip cream or some other exotic food and serve them as a topping for cake, pies or puddings. No cook or restaurant of today could equal the exquisite flavor of those concoctions.

I have noticed that there are few patches of wild strawberries in recent times. I am sure the regular burning of brush then contributed to the propagation of the wild strawberry plants.

PIGS IN PEN BELOW THE OLD BARN AT THE HARLAN RANCH

Circa 1930's

After the highway came through it was more common to keep the pigs penned up since they could easily get onto the highway and create a hazard. It should be noted that the pig trough in this picture is still of the old hollowed out redwood log style. The cross sticks were nailed onto the trough to encourage the pigs to space themselves out while feeding.

May 1944

NEIGHBORHOOD HELP AT A SPRING RODEO AT "SECTION 36"

May 1944

This scene was at our section 36 corral on the range between Vicente Creek and Big Creek. Dorman Thomas is on left; Marion Harlan next to him; Tony Fontis partly shielded by his horse, Domingo; Donald Harlan next to Tony. The individual at far right is George Harlan. The other person not identified.

ESTHER HARLAN AND ADA SMITH IN FLOWER GARDEN AT THE OLD HARLAN HOUSE WITH THE SMITH'S DOG, SKIPPER

My mother planted many different varieties of flowers in her garden at the ranch. Hollyhocks, scabiosa, columbines, sweet peas, snap dragons, nasturtiums, pansies, violets, cosmos, fox gloves, petunias, stocks, carnations and many others were her regular plantings. She saved and planted her own seed and bulbs and also shared with neighbors.

RIGDON'S MEMORIAL FOUNTAIN JUST NORTH OF GAMBOA POINT
Circa 1937

This was the location of one of the celebrations for the opening of Highway One in the summer of 1937. It is located just south of the point where the northern construction crew met the southern construction crew late in 1933. This was one of a number of fountains constructed along Highway One by the convict crews. The natural stone rock work is beautiful and rest rooms were available across the road on the ocean side. The State chose to close the facility because of the high cost upkeep of the rest rooms and the filtration of the spring water feeding the water fountain.

STANLEY WITH DIXIE IN SUMMER OF 1929

Dixie was a female dog that we had for a few years. We also had a male dog, Sport, who fathered two of Dixie's pups, Browny and Max, that we had as our ranch dogs through most of my "growing up" years. Max was later killed by an injured buck and he was replaced by a mixed breed pound dog named Shep. Sport died of old age and was replaced by another pound dog named Shorty.

STANLEY AT HIS GRADUATION FROM HIGH SCHOOL
IN PACIFIC GROVE IN JUNE OF 1946

Stanley also "boarded" with his aunts and grandmother in New Monterey during the time he was attending high school from 1942 to 1946. His interests in high school centered on woodworking and metalworking, athletics, and he also performed well in mathematics and the sciences. He served in the U S Army from1946 to 1948, then, completed a B A degree and teaching credentials at UCSB by August of 1952

ADA SMITH ON BABE AND MARIAN SMITH ON PINK
ON THE COAST TRAIL AT PLAN LATIGO

June 1937

This picture was taken as the family was returning home from a trout fishing trip in Vicente Creek. Vicente Creek was always a very productive stream for Rainbow trout. We seldom had to go more than a few holes above or below the trail crossing to limit out with trout. At that time the limit was 25 trout per individual. Local people made a special effort to transport the live small fish to locations upstream. By consistently doing this the stream produced nice size trout right up to the source springs.

STANLEY AND IRENE'S CHICKEN AND DUCK PEN
BELOW WHITE GUEST HOUSE AT RANCH

1948-49

Irene and I lived in my parent's white guest house on the ranch while Gene and I worked in the timber at Gamboas. I built this facility to house our ducks and chickens about 150 feet down the hill from the house. They responded by giving all the duck eggs and chicken eggs that we could use.

GENE WITH PIGS IN FIELD NEAR RANCHITO CREEK

1924

My father almost always had pigs on the ranch. They ranged freely in fenced regions of the ranch and upon maturity were encouraged to feed on the fall of tan oak and live oak acorns in Vicente Creek and adjacent hillsides.

After the highway came through in 1933, it was necessary to keep the pigs penned up so they wouldn't create a traffic hazard.

GENE, DONALD AND STANLEY ON THE BEACH AT MOSS LANDING

Christmas 1928

My mother was very close to her mother and two sisters who were living in Monterey at this time. It was traditional to visit one another on the holidays whenever possible. In 1928, it was necessary for us travel over the mountain by horseback to King City and then catch the train to Monterey. This was a two day venture. An alternative was to travel the Coast Trail to Big Sur with arrangements to meet our aunts who could come that far by automobile.

TWO COASTGUARD SEAMEN WITH THEIR COMMANDING
OFFICER AT OUR RANCHITO CABINS
Circa 1941-1945

ADA SMITH WITH MILK COW AND PIGS IN FIELD BY COON DITCH
Circa 1930

The ditch seen in the background was named by us for the frequent treeing of raccoons there by our dogs.

DONALD IN THE GARDEN ABOVE OUR OLD HOUSE
Circa 1928

All of us boys were intrigued by the machines and construction of Highway One. Moving dirt by any means was a great pastime for us. We sometimes emulated the convicts and their setting of dynamite charges. Our dynamite blasts were firecrackers, cherry bombs and blasting caps. As young adults we all "graduated" to using the real stuff. Don later held a Caltrans dynamite certificate.

DONALD, ESTHER AND STANLEY IN FIELD BETWEEN WINDMILL
AND COON DITCH

Spring 1928

It is hard to tell what the crop is that Donald and Esther are standing in. It could be pea vines. My mother was a great one to take advantage of every little patch of good soil for her gardens.

DONALD, GENE AND STANLEY ATOP BABE ON HILL VERY NEAR
OUR OLD HOUSE
Circa 1930

Babe was our favorite horse. She was very gentle and would put up with us doing anything around her. The barking dogs "Sport and Dixie" in this picture are being ignored by Babe.

Babe was called upon to do all sorts of specialty jobs around the ranch. The large radio antenna pole in the background was pulled nearly a mile by Babe from our redwood canyon to this location. She was then used to right the pole to a vertical position by use of long guy ropes. She followed verbal commands from my father without fault.

MY MOTHER, ESTHER HARLAN, ON THE FRONT PORCH OF OUR
FAMILY HOME
Circa 1940's

The bed on the front porch was a way in which my mother accommodated extra visitors at the Harlan ranch. Donald sometimes slept there, leaving his bedroom available for the aunts and our grandmother, Lucy Smith, when they visited in the summer.

GENE, ESTHER, DONALD AND STANLEY HARLAN

Summer 1928

This picture was taken in the garden just below the Harlan family home. My aunt Marian was teaching at Redwood School that year and very likely was the person who took the picture.

GENE HARLAN IN HIS "FORWARD BALL BEARING COASTER"
WAGON IN FRONT OF OUR OLD HOUSE

February 1928

Gene found limited areas where he could use his wagon. His favorite was to pull it up to the top of the hill by the radio pole and then point it downhill and ride it without precaution.

OUR OLD HOUSE AND GRANARY

January 1951

Gene and his family had been living in our old house from 1947 to 1949, then, my mother and father moved back in in 1949 while finishing their new house. In the mid and late 50's and 60's it was rented to the Houk family.

LUCY, ADA AND ESTHER HAULING BARLEY ON A SLED FROM
FIELD AT THE DEMAS PLACE
Circa 1918

*Barley was grown for feeding chickens and pigs by George and Esther Harlan
when they first started out at the Demas Place. It could also be stored in the barn
for feeding later in the fall and winter. Planted in early spring the barley would
mature by late June or July. After the scythed barley was raked and hauled to the
barn the pigs were allowed into the field to feed on the leftovers.*

*This must have been a rousing experience for Esther's sisters who had grown up in
Campbell and had not witnessed a great deal of farming or ranching. They did,
however, work in the fruit industry cutting and drying apricots and picking up
prunes that were commonly grown on the farms near their home.*

STANLEY IN PERAMBULATOR AT THE HARLAN RANCH

1928

My mother would push me down to her vegetable garden at some distance from the house. After working in the Garden for a few hours she would load up the space around me with vegetables and push me and the vegetables all the way back to the house. Donald was usually with us, but he had to walk all the way in both directions. The wheels were large enough in diameter to allow traveling over the rough ground, but it was not an easy task for my mother.

MARIAN SMITH ON JUANITA, JOHNNY MOY'S MULE, NEAR
BACKYARD GATE AT THE OLD HARLAN HOUSE

1928

*My aunt Marian taught at Redwood School from January 27, 1927 to June 3, 1927
and August 22, 1928 to June 8, 1929 when my mother was preoccupied with my
birth and early care. Marian stayed at our house while she was teaching and
made the one-mile trip to school each day with Gene who was in the 2nd or third
grade. Here she is shown on Juanita, a mule believed to be owned by Johnny Moy,
manager of the ranch at what is now known as Pacific Valley.*

REMNANTS OF THE FLUME AT MILL CREEK
Circa 1915

One of three saw mills that were located in Mill Creek (about 4 miles south of our ranch) built a flume to carry the finished lumber to the ocean where it was loaded onto a boat off shore. This photo shows the flume extending out across the beach. I once interviewed a student who went to school in Mill Creek and she related how she and other students rode the flume down to the beach after school hours on their way home. Drying off before going home was their greatest concern since their parents were not aware of their actions.

A GROUP OF EQUIDAE ON FREE RANGE NEAR GAMBOA POINT

1920's

In the early days of ranching along the Big Sur Coast it was common for each ranch to maintain a number of horses and mules and sometimes donkeys. Horses were used for transportation, plowing, pulling sleds or wagons, roundups, rodeos and many other applications. Both boys and girls of the large homestead families became experts at riding and roping.

**ESTHER HARLAN AND ADA SMITH AT THE BEACH ON A
FISHING OUTING**

Easter 1954

*My mother enjoyed fishing off the rocky shoreline throughout her life at Lopez
Point. There were certain holes that were favorites of us all for producing fish.
There were a number of different varieties of fish that could be caught in this area.
Bull Heads (Cabezone), brown cod, soreos (kelp cod), sea trout, rainbow perch
and an occasional ling cod were most common. A poke pole (as seen behind my
mother) with a short piece of chalk line and a number 6/0 hook, at the small end,
was used to fish underneath the large rocks along the shoreline. Fishing was
usually best on an incoming tide with overcast skies. Fishing in the small bays off
shore could be accomplished with a long chalk line (throw line) with a similar
hook and sinker (rock) attached to the outer end with excess line wrapped around
a shingle.*

MARIAN SMITH WITH DONKEY NEAR RADIO POLE AT OLD HOUSE

Early 1920's

I don't remember my father having a donkey, but many of the families in the area did have. Manuel Lopez was said to have a number of them when he was living on the coast. The donkey was much smaller than a mule or a horse, but they survived the winter with less food than their counterparts.

A DAY AT LIME KILN BEACH FOR THE HARLANS
Circa 1929

Horses could be ridden all the way to the sand beach at the mouth of Lime Kiln Creek via the Coast Trail and the wagon road that had been used by the lime kiln company to reach Rockland Landing as seen at top of picture. It became a popular spot for all of the families along this part of the coast for picnics. This beach can be dangerous in stormy weather.

COAST GURDSMAN BILL CHAMBERLAIN IN FULL BATTLE GEAR
NEAR THE LOOKOUT ON THE HARLAN PROPERTY

1943

Bill Chamberlain and my brother, Donald, got along very well. They hunted and fished together and also took the dory at Big Creek out for off shore adventures. I once accompanied them on one of these trips and ended up soaking wet on the sand beach a half mile south of Big Creek. I walked back to Big Creek along the beach!

COAST GUARDSMAN RAYMOND BOND IN DRESS UNIFORM
WHILE SERVING AT LOPEZ POINT
Circa 1943

Raymond Bond was one of many guardsmen who served at Lopez Point during World War Two years. After his assignment at Lopez Point he kept in touch with my mother for many years by mail.

GROUP OF FAMILY AND FRIENDS ON HILL NEAR GEORGE AND
ESTHER HARLAN'S OLD HOUSE
Circa 1928

Johnny Moy, Marian Smith, Lulu Harlan, Hester Harlan Kiplinger Victorine standing. Edwin Kiplinger, Donald Harlan, Gene Harlan and Opal Kiplinger seated. Johnny was a friend of Marian and Lulu and Hester were sisters of my father. Hester sometimes stayed with us at the ranch when my mother was off attending teacher's institute which was a yearly requirement of all public school teachers in the County.

WATER TROUGH BELOW THE OLD HARLAN HOME
Circa 1940's

This trough was supplied from a small spring in the ditch behind the Harlan house. The water was allowed to run freely into the trough with the overflow maintaining a good stand of water cress. It served stock in two different ranges above the highway. Note the two ducks in the trough. These were pet ducks brought to the ranch by Marian and Ada Smith on their usual visit to the Harlans during the summer months.

STANLEY, DONALD AND GENE IN THE TIDEPOOL AT THE
MOUTH OF THE CREEK
Circa 1930

Our family made frequent trips to the beach during the summer. This pool was pretty well surrounded by large rocks and at a moderate tide, and a summer calm, it was quite safe. Wading was an accepted activity and later we actually attempted to swim in this pool. We never did become efficient swimmers here because of the extremely cold water. As the tide came in we found it to be quite productive for fishing.

STANLEY AND DONALD NEAR PORCH STEPS AT THE HARLAN HOME

Spring 1928

My mother was able to push, or pull, the perambulator over the rough ground quite well. She took me along with her to the garden nearly a quarter mile away from the house. I whiled away the hours as she worked in the garden, then I was pushed back up the hill to the house along with a selection of vegetables for use in the kitchen.

TD14 GETTING NEW RING AND PINION GEARS BY GENE HARLAN
AT 36 FIELD ON ROAD BUILDING TO THE MARBLE PLACE

1947

Gene Harlan worked for my father and John Nesbitt in building many miles of roads on Circle M Ranch. He built the present graded road from the highway up to the ranch house replacing the very steep and narrow road which had existed since the early 1930's. He also built most of the road connecting the Circle M ranch house with Avilas, French Camp, Gamboas, Big Creek, The Marble Place and Section 36.

Mr. Nesbitt bought the new TD14 from military surplus after the war for use on his ranch. Gene was the primary operator in the years 1946 through 1948. The TD14 was equipped with a Bucyrus Erie bulldozer blade which, for its time, was a very efficient road constructing machine.

ESTHER AND GEORGE HARLAN IN MONTEREY VISITING THE
SMITHS AT 746 CYPRESS STREET

December 1956

*My mother was very close to her two sisters and her mother. Once the highway
was opened to public use they made frequent trips to Monterey for supplies and to
carry out other ranch business.*

FRED HARLAN WITH LARGE RATTLESNAKE ENCOUNTERED ON
A TROUT FISHING TRIP TO LOST VALLEY

Summer 1932

My aunts, along with George and Esther, would go on trout fishing trips by horseback to the back country of Big Creek and other mountain streams. Fred and Marion Harlan sometimes would also go along. They sometimes caught larger fish by going to less frequented areas. Rattlesnakes were prevalent in these areas.

GEORGE AND ESTHER HARLAN'S WHITE GUEST HOUSE

1948

George Harlan built this structure, with the help of Mervin Merit from the King City area, in the early 1930's. Materials for it were brought in by a launch from Monterey and delivered to our beach at Lopez Point. Most of the materials were hand carried from the beach to the building site. I remember carrying one end of the half inch water pipe up the steep trail. The building was intended to be the new school house situated closer to the new highway. My mother was teaching in our family home during this time and the new school was built, also by my father, very near the highway in section 17 instead. The White House was rented, first to the Coberlys and later to the Cortners, as a temporary home while the highway and bridges were being built. After 1938 we used it as a guest house for visitors and other family members. It burned to the ground in the 1985 Rat Creek Fire.

ESTHER, ADA AND MARIAN WITH THE SMITH'S DOG MACKIE
ON MOUNT HAMILTON IN THE EARLY 1960'S

Gene Harlan was employed by the University of California and lived in housing the University provided on top of the mountain. He was employed as a machinist, and later, as an assistant astronomer. This picture was taken on a visit to see Gene and his family while they were living on top of Mount Hamilton. It was rare that all three sisters were in the same picture. Virginia completed her high school education in Los Gatos about the time the family moved to the top of the mountain. Beverly, Virginia's sister, attended school on Mount Hamilton. She later completed her education at UCSC.

HARLAN RANGE CATTLE GRAZING ON "36" FIELD WITH
THE GAMBOA PINES IN THE BACKGROUND

1940's

George Harlan raised oat hay on the field in the foreground for a number of years in the 1940's. The range land above the fence and all that seen in the background was used for grazing the year round. He maintained a corral at the far end of the field beyond the near hill on the right. We first hauled the loose hay to our barns on the home ranch by truck. We later experimented with a baling machine which was stationary and the hay had to be delivered to it for baling. This required a number of people to operate. Two people had to deliver the hay, another had to feed the baler and another had to insert divider boards, thread and tie the wire on the bales and stack the finished ones. The bales still had to be loaded on the truck by hand and hauled to the barn.

ADA, GENE, MARIAN AND GARDENER JACOBSEN IN THE
BACK YARD BY THE OLD HARLAN HOUSE
Circa 1925

*This picture shows a good catch of fish and red abalone at the George and Esther
Harlan ranch. Gardener was staying with Mrs. Stiverson at the Ranchito while
teaching school at Redwood School from 1924 to 1926.*

GEORGE HARLAN HITCHING UP THE TEAM OF HORSES TO THE
SPRING WAGON NEAR THE WAGON CAVE
Circa 1916

*The spring wagon was kept under the overhanging rock of the cave. It was
necessary to back the wagon up a sloped embankment in front of the cave to get it
in place. In this scene it looks as though George has just brought the wagon out of
the cave with his team of horses and is headed into town (King City), possibly on
his way to be married in Campbell to Esther in 1916.*

ADA RIDING BAREBACK ON OUR HORSE, TRIXIE AND MARIAN
ALSO RIDING BAREBACK ON BABE
Circa 1926

Ada and Marian, sisters of Esther Harlan, loved to visit at the Harlan ranch. They participated in all activities that were at hand. Here, they have just brought Trixie and Babe in from their pasture to be saddled for an excursion of some sort.

GEORGE AND ESTHER HARLAN'S GREAT GRANDSON, DAVID
WOOD, WITH DONALD'S PONY, LADY, AT DEER FLAT

May 1991

After George and Esther had passed on, their great grandson, David, enjoyed going to the ranch and helping out with all of the chores relating to animal and ranch upkeep. Here he is enjoying an exercise walk of Don's pony, around the loop trail above the ranch house.

The 1985 Rat Creek Fire created the bare limbs in the background. Most of the redwood trees in our canyon experienced a searing heat and exploded into fire, all of the way to the top, leaving only skeleton outlines of the trees and limbs. Grasses flourished in the ashes after the fire and some of the redwoods sprouted new growth as seen here in this photo.

ESTHER AND GEORGE HARLAN OBSERVING STEAM VENTS
AT YELLOWSTONE NATIONAL PARK

Early 1960's

In their later years George and Esther did some well-earned travelling with Esther's sisters, Ada and Marian Smith. They toured most of the western states and took in the well-known national parks. Both of them enjoyed these summer outings.

Stanley and Irene Harlan, along with their daughter, Carmen, stayed at the ranch on these occasions and took care of the routine chores that are always a part of ranching. Carmen especially enjoyed feeding the animals and riding, with the Harlan dogs, in the jeep to the far reaches of the cattle ranges

ESTHER AND GEORGE HARLAN OBSERVING THE NACIMIENTO
DAM SITE ON THE NACIMIENTO RIVER

Summer 1963

My father was very interested in developments that would improve the ranching and farming industries of Monterey County. He marveled at the accomplishments at both the Nacimiento and the San Antonio dam sites and the impounding of winter run-off waters that could be used for irrigation in the Salinas Valley. My father had swum the Nacimiento River, with his string of horses and pack mules, a number of times in his efforts to deliver the mail from Jolon to the Lucia Post Office on the coast.

ESTHER HARLAN SITTING ON HER HIDE-A-BED IN HER LIVING
ROOM OPENING HER MANY GIFTS AT CHRISTMAS TIME

1962

Esther enjoyed both giving and receiving gifts on holidays for the family. It was traditional for the extended family to gather at the ranch during the Christmas holidays. Esther put on an exquisite dinner of many main courses and additional deserts of many kinds. Other family members helped with the preparation, serving and clean-up but my mother did most of the cooking herself. Cooking was one of her favorite pastimes.

CHRISTMAS DINNER AT THE GEORGE AND ESTHER HARLAN HOME

Christmas 1962

George is seen in the foreground left and Esther at near right. Traditionally the family would gather at the Harlan ranch at Christmas time. Here you see tables set up in the living room area to accommodate the large number of guests present. My mother always made each dinner an historical event. An excellent cook, she provided more food than anyone could possibly eat.

GEORGE AND ESTHER HARLAN ON DOLAN RIDGE WITH THE BACK COUNTRY OF BIG CREEK IN THE BACKGROUND—

The range north of Big Creek could accommodate approximately fifty head of adult cows and two bulls. My father and Donald built a jeep access road to the range from a point on the highway just north of Big Creek Point with our TD9 bulldozer. The range had no corral when he first started grazing cattle on this area. It was necessary to drive the cattle he used for stocking on the highway for over four miles which created a number of problems with tourists. To alleviate these, he built a corral and loading chute just off the highway at the road heading. In spite of lion problems, he ranged cattle here until 1969, a year after Esther died. We also ranged a few head of cattle on Mining Ridge, part of which is seen at far right, during this era as well.

ONE OF GEORGE HARLAN'S SOWS CROSSED WITH SIBERIAN
WILD BOAR

Early 1980's

George found that pigs with Siberian blood could protect their young against coyotes and most mountain lions. He allowed them to run free on the range and most of the sows were able to raise their young to maturity. He fed them daily with food scraps, barley and corn. In addition, they were able to forage for acorns, thistles, grass and other foodstuffs better than full blooded domestic pigs. He raised these breeds for nearly 20 years—1965 to his death in 1985. He sometimes sold them at auction and at other times took orders from private individuals for young, lean and well-fed pork.

FIRE IN BEE CAMP AND THE HEADWATERS OF BIG CREEK
AS SEEN FROM DONNIE'S RIDGE

1950's

Wild fires have always been a concern for the people who lived in the Santa Lucia Mountains. They realized, early in their experiences, that fire could eliminate the animal feed, reduce their picket fences to ashes, incinerate their homes and even burn them and their animals to death under certain conditions. They took precautions by burning areas of brush in the winter time when a wild fire was unlikely, thereby creating fire breaks for an uncontrolled fire in the dry summer and fall months. They backfired down the canyons to eliminate the dead leaves and limbs. When necessary, they fought the fire with only basic tools. Nearly all homesteads and mature trees survived until the massive Rat Creek fire of 1985 when all was lost.

ESTHER HARLAN WITH HER THREE GRANDDAUGHTERS ON THE
FRONT DECK OF HER HOME AT LOPEZ POINT
Circa 1956

MISTY, GEORGE HARLAN'S CATTLE DOG, CHECKING OUT A
TREE SQUIRREL THAT SHE HAD RUN UP A TREE

Misty was a puppy in 1968 when my mother died. My mother named her Misty because of her fine white and gray/blue hair. She kept my father company for number of years in the late 1960's and into the 1970's. She was a natural born cattle dog and did many things for my father that he could no longer do with his crippled legs. She rode in the back of his pickup wherever he travelled. Her alertness to changing events and dangers helped my father be aware of his surroundings in his elder years.

TYPICAL RANGE COW AND CALF ON THE HARLAN RANCH
NEAR THE LIGHTNING TREE ON SECTION 8

Spring 1988

This well-fed cow and her calf are a typical example of the Aberdeen Angus breed that my father developed over the years. When he first started ranching on a large scale he was only able to stock the ranges with various breeds. As time passed, he always bought registered Angus bulls for breeding purposes. This controlled breeding, brought out the best qualities in the range herds. He also introduced some Brown Swiss through one of his milk cows, and, as this example shows, the brown tint in the calf's coat signifies this blood cross. The Brown Swiss breed had a very gentle nature and reduced the "wild" nature of some of the early Harlan stock. Round-ups in the early days were a major event that challenged all of our abilities to gather in the cattle to the various corrals.

A VIEW DUE NORTH FROM THE HARLAN HOME SHOWING THE
WHITE GUEST HOUSE AND STANLEY'S WORKSHOP

1950's

*This house, originally built by George Harlan, with the help of Mervin Merritt in
the early 1930's, was intended for use as Redwood Branch School. Plans changed
when the highway was being constructed in 1933 and another sight was selected in
section 17. The Harlans used this home for an overflow for guests or family
members over the years. Stanley and Irene Harlan lived here from the spring of
1948 until September of 1949. The house and workshop burned to the ground in
the 1985 Rat Creek Fire.*

RANGE CATTLE GRAZING ON THE BIG FLAT AT LOPEZ POINT

Fall 1985

This group represented the survivors of the July 1985 Rat Creek Fire. A number of our stock were killed or seriously burned in this fire along with dozens of deer and other animals. A resident flock of approximately 100 crows were all killed in this fire, and to this date, in 2010, they have not reestablished themselves. The area below the highway was not burned and served as a grazing area and feed yard until the spring rains came in 1986 when our cattle could return to the open range. A number of the animals seen in this picture had very serious feet, facial and udder burns that they never recovered from. We, the Harlans, have felt this fire was the result of Government restrictions on our traditional winter burning of excess fuels that had accumulated for a number of years since the 1940's when these restrictions became evident.

GEORGE HARLAN SITTING ALONG SIDE HIS CHEVROLET PICKUP
IN THE YARD BY HIS HOME

December 17, 1983

George searched out the warm and sunny spots in his later years. He was already 90 years old in this picture.

HARLAN RANGE CATTLE GRAZING ON THE OLD BORONDA
HOMESTEAD SITE IN SECTION 7

May 1966

This part of the range was a favorite resting spot for many animals. It was high enough in elevation to be above the coastal fog most of the time. Corrals were maintained here from the time my father first ranged cattle on this land after the Borondas sold to Edward S. Moore and then moved away in about 1928. Access to this area by motor vehicle did not occur until the Harlans constructed a roadway in the late 1940's. Considerable work was done by Donald Harlan to develop natural springs and create year-round watering troughs for the cattle and other animals. My father fed his open range pigs here for a number of years.

A SCENE OF RANGE LAND IN SECTION 8 ALONG THE BORONDA
SCHOOL TRAIL

May 1966

The slight mark of the trail is seen in the lower left portion of the photograph. The Boronda children used this trail daily in traveling to Redwood School. In more recent times the cattle used it to travel across the canyons and ditches from one grassy ridge to another. There is a good watering spring in Lopez Canyon located under the tall redwood trees at the center of the picture. A layer of fog can be seen at the lower elevation—very typical in the late spring and summer months for this area.

GENE, IRENE, STANLEY AND DONALD HARLAN IN STANLEY'S
BACK YARD IN MONTEREY

September 2, 1981

It was rare for all three of the Harlan sons to be photographed as a group. This gathering occurred for the wedding celebration of Carmen Harlan and John Wood in Monterey on this date. Gene worked as a machinist after high school graduation, then he worked for the University of California on Mount Hamilton as a machinist and an assistant astronomer. Stanley served in the army for 2 years in the occupation forces in Germany, then taught high school Industrial Arts for 32 years. Donald also served two years in the Army on Adak, Alaska then worked for Cal Trans from 1956 to 1985, first as a maintenance employee, then as a maintenance foreman. All three of them worked off and on at the home ranch when opportunity or conditions allowed it

THE WATERFALL ON THE HARLAN RANCH LOCATED VERY NEAR
THE WHITE GUEST HOUSE IN THE BIG FLAT CREEK

Spring 1974

No record of the Harlan Ranch at Lopez Point would be complete without this scene of the water falling gracefully into the pool below. This large a flow is typical of a normal year in the late spring months. Dry years may not produce an actual fall of water. Extremely wet years can produce a phenomenal flow covering the complete wall of rock and even overflow into another channel on the left.

THE GAMBOA RANGE AS SEEN FROM SECTION 6 ACROSS
VICENTE CREEK

May 1966

This was part of the range that my father grazed cattle on for a number of years. It extended from Vicente Creek on the south to Big Creek on the north and from the highway near the ocean to the forest boundary on the east. It was the largest of the ranges and could support as many as 70 head of adult cattle. We maintained corrals at Palos Quatros and Section 36 field. Vehicle access was only to the section 36 corral. There was good water distribution on this range from natural springs and also from either major creek where cattle could gain access. The herd on this range included three bulls. Most of this range was originally owned by the Gamboa family until sold to Marion Hollins and Edward Small Moore in the late 1920's.

LOOKING NORTH FROM THE DOLAN DAIRY TOWARD RAT
CANYON AND EAGLE ROCK

May 1966

This was the northernmost part of the range that my father grazed cattle on. It was bordered by the north fork of Big Creek on the south, Rat Canyon on the north, the highway to the west and the U S Forest to the east. This range could accommodate approximately 50 head of adult cattle and was served by two bulls. Phillip Dolan, known to have worked harder than any of the homestead pioneers to clear his land, created much of this open grassland from brushy thickets. His wife and children moved from the coast to other property, near Moss Landing, so the children could attend school. Phillip stayed on the coast for a number of additional years, working like a slave and living a hermit's life. This part of the property was purchased by Moore.

THE JUAN BAUTISTA AVILA HOMESTEAD HOUSE

Early 1980's

Juan Bautista Avila homesteaded the NW ¼ of section 9 adjacent to the homestead of my great grandfather, Gabriel Dani. A large family was raised here and the children attended Redwood School. This location, between Lime Kiln Creek and Vicente Creek, was within the southern most range that my father grazed cattle on. Donald Harlan's horse, Sulay, is in this picture with Donald looking out the window opening. The picture was taken more than 50 years after the Avilas moved away from the coast. One of Juan's sons, Steve, was a noted lion hunter in the area and my father called on him when depredation of his calves occurred. This historical location burned to the ground in the Rat Creek Fire of July 1985.

THE RANCHITO FIELD AS SEEN FROM THE FENCE LINE OF
THE GEORGE HARLAN PROPERTY

May 1966

The Ranchito Field was homesteaded by Pedro Lopez, one of the Lopez's sons, and upon his early death the homestead was occupied by Santos Boronda, son of Jose De Los Santos Boronda. The property was sold to the Gamboas by the Lopez family and then was sold to Edward S. Moore to become a part of Circle M Ranch. A teacher of Redwood School; Mary Stiverson with her son, Otis, and two other school age children, Arthur and Gardener Jacobson; lived here for a two-year period from 1924 to 1926. My father used this field in the 1930's and 1940's for pasturing his stallion, Bunch. It was in this field that my father's angora billy goat chased my brother, Donald, and me into the old barn, which was located here, after we had made a run with our dogs at the group of nannies and kids.

CARMEN IN THE CORRAL FEEDING CORN STALKS TO A GROUP
OF CALVES BEING WEANED FROM THEIR MOTHERS

November 1963

This was one of Carmen's favorite activities when she would go to the ranch with her parents. My father would usually hold back a few head of heifers for restocking the older cows each year. It was necessary to separate the calves from their mothers for a two or three-week period of time so they would not go back to nursing when returned to the range. Since these were to be the future cows on the ranch it was desirable to gentle them down as much as possible. Carmen's efforts were much appreciated by my father. The sweet green corn suckers from my mother's garden suited the calves perfectly. It did not take long for them to become real pets.

A GROUP OF GRAZING CATTLE IN BOROND'S FIELD

Spring 1977

The Jose de los Santos Boronda family homesteaded 160 acres in section 7, including this parcel, in the late 1800's. His homestead became valid (was proven) on October 13, 1893. He and his second wife raised a large family here. Their youngest child, Julia, graduated from Redwood School in June of 1928. The property was sold to Edward Small Moore soon after that date.

At the left center of the picture one of my father's sows is eating green grass and leading her piglets toward the feeding trough. Though very gentle and trustworthy to my father, this sow could explode into a violent warrior if her pigs were threatened by coyotes or mountain lions. Her blood lines are part Siberian boar.

ESTHER WITH HER GRANDDAUGHTER, CARMEN, ON CARMEN'S
GRADUATION DAY FROM HIGH SCHOOL

June 1968

Esther was very approving to see her granddaughters achieve well in school. Sadly, she did not see Carmen or her granddaughter Beverly go on to finish college. She died just 4 months after this photograph was taken.

Stanley, an Industrial Arts Teacher at Watsonville High School, saw Carmen complete her education through H.A. Hyde Elementary School, E. A. Hall Junior High School and Watsonville High School. She then went on to Cabrillo Junior College and finished her B. A. and teaching credentials, as her grandmother had done, at California State University at San Jose.

ESTHER'S GARDEN IN THE AREA BETWEEN THE HOUSE AND THE
BARN

1960's

My mother was a great gardener. She sometimes had 3 or 4 different gardens going all at the same time. She always had flowers around the house and grew vegetables on every available plot. Here she has corn, squash, beans, peas, peppers, tomatoes, carrots, beets and cucumbers to name a few. Gophers, squirrels, rabbits and deer were always a challenge to keep under control.

GEORGE HARLAN'S CATTLE GRAZING NEAR THE OLD MINE
ON THE RANGE NORTH OF BIG CREEK

1960's

This range was originally part of the Phillip Dolan holdings. Not far from this spot he maintained a dairy where he milked cows and processed the milk into cheese. He had other property in the Moss Landing area where he acquired dairy stock and drove them over the mountain to his ranch on the coast. His route from the Salinas Valley was up the Arroro Seco River to Lost Valley and then over the top of the mountain at Bee Camp and down past Eagle Rock and onto Dolan Ridge. Many of his stock were day old male dairy breeds which were given to him for free. He fed them on milk until they were old enough to wean, then he drove them over the mountain to the coast. He lost many of them to the rough terrain and some even went wild on the return trip.

GEORGE HARLAN HOLDING AN AWARD HE RECEIVED FROM THE
MARINE CORPS

August 1977

On July 1, 1977 a Marine Corps Navy helicopter, piloted by Commander P. F. Duffy, had mechanical trouble and landed on my father's field (The Big Flat at Lopez Point). No one was injured on the emergency landing, but it was necessary to make repairs to the helicopter before it was airworthy and could take off on its own power.

My father willingly gave them access through his gates and property to make the repairs, which they seemed overly thankful for. A few weeks later they delivered this plaque to him in thanks for his cooperation. Another occurrence was by three Marine Corpse surveillance aircraft when one ran out of fuel. A private plane with four occupants landed there in the 1930's with a serious oil leak and they also were able to take off, with only the pilot, after repairs.

GEORGE HARLAN RESTING IN HIS LIVING ROOM

April 1971

GEORGE HARLAN ATTENDING ONE OF HIS COWS WITH NEWLY
BORN TWIN CALVES

July 1968

*Twin calves are quite a rarity with range cattle and because the cow only wants to
identify with the last born problems can develop. Sometimes the mother will not
accept both of them under any circumstances and, undetected, the older calf will
simply starve to death. Solutions are varied. One is to keep the calves separate
from the mother for a few hours, then tie the cow up with a rope in the corral and
let both calves nurse. This technique to be repeated for a period two weeks then
see if she accepts both calves. If not, then foster one calf to another more
agreeable cow. Sometimes it is necessary to hand feed the calf with a nursing
bottle and finally a bucket until it is able to survive on grass alone.*

A HARLAN COW 45 DAYS AFTER EXPOSURE TO THE RAT CREEK FIRE

July - August 1985

Of a total herd of 40 head this badly burned cow survived the holocaust of the fire only to be sent to market a few months later because of serious damage to her udder. She was no longer able to nurse a new-born calf. Besides the outright death of 5 head of cows there were another five who suffered hoof damage and other serious burns that necessitated their being put down. My brother, Donald, hand fed this cow for many weeks after the fire to insure that she regained her strength. He aptly named her "CRISP". There were a few head that suffered no burns and others that suffered minor burns that allowed recovery. The mid-summer timing of this fire combined with hot dry weather and a collection of many years of heavy fuels made this fire very disastrous to our cattle, wildlife and forest trees as well.

A FOREST OF MIXED OAK AND MADRONE TREES BURNED BEYOND
RECOGNITION A DAY AFTER THE FIRE

July 1985

Nearly all of the large trees were lost in this fire of July 1985, known as the Rat Creek Fire. The heat was intense, and the bark of the trees could not protect the cambium layer as it would in a less intense fire. Many large oak trees, centuries old, later rotted and fell to the ground. Redwood trees, noted for their ability to experience and survive a fire, flamed up like roman candles in many locations. Though many of them re-sprouted in the months following the fire there were many others that lost their limbs and turned into white ghosts of the forest. All of the Hoover's Manzanitas, noted for their large size in this area, were killed outright. It will take nearly a century of "proper" management for these trees to recover to their original stature.

ONE OF GEORGE HARLAN'S TOP QUALITY BLACK ANGUS HEIFERS IN
THE CORRAL NEAR THE BARN

November 1963

This animal posed for the camera and became the silhouette for the weather vane that Stanley made for the ranch house roof top. It remained there for at least 44 years until a violent wind twisted the leg supports and sent it asunder. I should have used thicker metal on the leg sections. Possibly it will be repaired in the future.

My father always held back some of his best proportioned and gentlest heifers for restocking purposes. Most range cows showed signs of old age at 10 and were replaced with younger stock. The older cows did not winter over well and became thin and weak. If kept into old age, many of them would be lost in ditches or over the ocean bank due to slipping and falling.

IRENE, GEORGE, CARMEN AND MISTY IN DONALD'S 1946 JEEP

Fall 1973

Irene and Carmen are seen here holding a large string of rockfish taken from the shoreline at Lopez Point. Cabezone seemed to be the most common fish caught here. Ling Cod, as seen at the right end of the string, seemed to be plentiful, but they favored a full-sized squid to take the bait. Other varieties were Rainbow Perch, Brown Cod, Sea Trout and Kelp Cod (Sorreos). All were fine eating and enjoyed by the Harlans throughout their stay here. Donald's jeep was a handy vehicle to use on the ranch. It's short wheel base and narrow stance, along with its four-wheel drive, was a favorite for of all of us on or off the road. My father used it to carry feed to his pigs in good weather or when his pickup was in need of repairs. Donald performed most of the mechanical repairs on the pickup, tractors, truck, light plant and other machines on the ranch.

LOOKING DOWN ON THE GEORGE AND ESTHER HARLAN HOME
FROM THE ROAD DIRECTLY ABOVE THE HOUSE

March 1987

This photograph shows how the house was built into the ridge top with a terraced effect at each level. All of us had some hand in building this structure in the late 1940's. We all helped in hauling sand and gravel from 36 beach to make the concrete. We also all helped in the mixing and wheel barrowing the concrete to its destination in the various forms for the rock walls, the foundations, etc. A small 3 cu. Ft. mixer with a Briggs and Stratton engine did all the actual mixing. Stanley left for Santa Barbara in September of 1949 to attend UCSB. Gene left the coast also about this time since he had acquired a job with Los Gatos Construction Company. George and Donald were left to complete the house with brief hired help from Mr. Roy Kenworthy.
The shingles are of redwood from Big Creek and were split and re-sawed to order by Wid Dayton.

LOOKING DOWN ONTO THE RANCH FIELDS AND LOPEZ ROCK
FROM THE TOP OF THE GOAT ROCK

March 1987

This view shows the north end of the Harlan fields below the highway, the top of the Goat Rock in the foreground and Lopez Rock approximately ½ mile offshore. The black strip on the field is the result of Donald and Gene's attempt to keep the brush in tow with the bulldozer and disk. The light streaks in the water are caused by a rough ocean eroding the clay slides off the ocean bank from the previous winter rains. The contrast in the ocean colors is somewhat unusual.

Results of the 1985 Rat Creek Fire is still evident on the side hill of lilacs on the right and in some low bushes in the foreground. Note the bare black limbs of the dead trees.

LOOKING DOWN ON THE OLD HARLAN HOME COMPLEX FROM THE "TOP OF THE HILL" AS IT APPEARD IN APRIL OF 1963

Our old house was still being lived in at this time. The elderly Houks were paying my mother a token rental for their stay there. The house, granary, and barn with its attached pig shed were still standing at this time. The relocated chicken house is just out of the picture on the right directly above the old house. Encroachment of brush onto the fields is evident in this picture. My father was getting along in years and was unable to keep up with the constant battle of grubbing out the lupines, greasewoods and other chaparral. It must have been hard on him to see all of the hard work he had devoted to clearing the land be overtaken again by the returning brush. This picture was taken before the few natural ditches in the fields were filled by the highway slide removal crews.

252

LOOKING DOWN ONTO THE HARLAN FIELDS FROM THE ROAD
ABOVE THE OLD HOUSE NEAR THE WATER TROUGH

March 1987

This scene shows the work that Donald and Gene had been doing with the bulldozer and the disk to eradicate the encroaching brush in the fields. My father had passed on 18 months earlier and Donald was staying on the ranch at this time. Don and Gene's efforts were very effective at ridding the fields of brush but the side hills were too steep to handle in a similar fashion. Donald also devoted the last 20 years of his life at hand grubbing the ginesta (French broom) and other unwanted varieties on the ranch in areas where the bulldozer could not be used due to steepness of the terrain. Note that in this photo the original natural ditches have been filled with highway slide overburden and an extensive storm run-off collection system was built with its concrete drain installed across the field.

ONE OF GEORGE HARLAN'S PIGS EATING CORN NEAR THE FEED
TROUGH

June 1975

This is a typical example of the pigs my father raised in his later years. The shadow of his hat is outlined on the ground near the pig. The mothers had sufficient Siberian blood to make them a formidable enemy of any coyote or mountain lion that would attempt to take one of their piglets.

I had the first-hand experience of finding a dead sow of my father's that had been wounded earlier by a lumber mill employee and left to die. Evidently a lion made an attempt to finish off the wounded sow and ended up with the front paw in the sow's grip of her teeth. I found both badly decayed but with unmistakable evidence of what had occurred. The rest of the lion was not in the area.

ONE OF MY FATHER'S PIGS WITH NOTABLY CURLY HAIR

April 1964

No two pigs were exactly the same as this animal indicates. There were color variations and body proportion variations just as it might be with other animal groups. The pigs that my father raised had sufficient Siberian blood to give them two coats of hair or fur. Close to the skin was a layer of very fine fur and then the courser hair on the outside. I butchered many of my father's pigs for individual buyers and observed many traits that I was not aware of before. I am sure there was much inbreeding because the same wild boars usually bred my father's sows. I was surprised to find the sexual makeup varying to a great extent. At least 10 % of the ones I slaughtered had variations in sexual organs. They varied from unmistakably male to unmistakably female with all variations in between.

GEORGE HARLAN'S DOG, SPROUT, WAITING FOR INSTRUCTIONS
AT A ROAD INTERSECTION

March 1987

Sprout was the last dog that my father had at the ranch. She was a true cattle dog and did not require much training to help my father with his cattle. Like most dogs, she learned to enjoy the rides in the back of my father's four wheel drive Chevrolet pickup. At my father's passing in 1985 she was left with my brother, Donald. Gene had come to the ranch on vacation from his job a short time before this picture was taken. He had cleaned the near level spot in foreground and planted barley on it. The dark green is a vigorous growth of barley which later matured into a field of grain. This spot on the ranch has been named "Gene's Patch" as a result of his efforts.

THE WEATHER VANE ON GEORGE AND ESTHER HARLAN'S HOME

Stanley originally constructed this weather vane from a sheet of stainless steel and mounted it on the house. Its outline was traced from a picture of one of his father's living weaner calves which showed outstanding characteristics of the Aberdeen Angus breed.

Winds here can reach 80 miles per hour before a storm front moves in on the area, and the thickness of the steel in the leg areas proved to be too weak for the forces exerted on it. It succumbed to the forces of nature on a couple of occasions. This picture was taken of it after the cupola was repaired and the mounting for the weather vane redone in May of 2006.

ESTHER HARLAN'S TROPICANA ROSES

May 2005

Esther was always proud of the flower gardens that she developed over the years. She planted these patented Tropicana Roses in her garden soon after the house was built. After her death in 1968, family survivors continued to care for the plants. Stanley added redwood sawdust and mushroom compost to the soil about the time this picture was taken, and they flourished into beautiful examples in the years following.

A YOUNG BLACK HEIFER TOYING WITH DONALD'S DOG, TERRY

June 12, 2005

Terry and the calves developed a game that they played regularly. Terry would lay down and act disinterested in the calves, then, when one came over to smell him, he would come to life instantly and respond by snapping at the calf's ears. The calves and Terry obviously enjoyed this little game and would replay it as long as we were in the area.

Donald purchased Terry, a Giant Rat Terrier, as a puppy from a person who lived in the area east of Paso Robles in 1999. His birthday was July 4, 1999. He lived an ideal dog's life at the ranch for the first five years until Donald passed on. Stanley and Irene have taken over his care since then.

CLOSE-UP OF A GENTLE BLACK ANGUS CALF

August 6, 2005

THE OLD HARLAN HOME AS IT LOOKED ON THIS DATE

May 10, 2006

Unoccupied, the old house fell to ruin in a relatively short period of time. Rose Houk had planted some cypresses and a redwood tree below the house when she lived there. They were well watered from the mud spring which had always existed there and they grew into giants in a short time. The old willow tree at the back of the house also prospered to the point where it almost engulfed the whole house. Hippie types made their overnight stay there on occasion and used the structure for their firewood. We had often thought of possibly rebuilding the structure to its original configuration and making a historical museum of it. County restrictions and the passage of time discouraged us from doing so.

YOUNG HARLAN ABERDEEN ANGUS CALVES

December 1992

At about this time each year we would gather the cattle into one of the corrals and perform vaccinations to the young calves against potential threats of illnesses that were proven to exist from one source or another. Black leg was a number one concern. The spores can live in the soil for years and is found all over the World. The spores can enter the calf's body by being ingested then it is transferred through the intestines causing almost immediate death to the animal. The young and most robust animals are the most susceptible to the disease. My father always felt the turkey buzzards came up from Mexico in the spring and transferred the deathly spores from there to here.

We would also place circulation restricting rubbers on the bull calves to eliminate the testicles and mark the right and left ears of each calf with the Harlan identity cut.

THE HARLAN HOME AS SEEN FROM THE JEEP ROAD ABOVE THE HOUSE—LOPEZ ROCK IN THE BACKGROUND

This picture was taken while repairs and painting were being done to the southeast wall. The house was built in 1949 and 1950 after George and Esther completed their three year stay at the Nesbitt ranch house. My mother enjoyed many of the modern conveniences that were included in the new home construction. She held many social gatherings here with neighbors and her Ladies Aid Club. Her stay at the old house was approximately 26 years where she raised her three boys. Her stay here was approximately 18 years. She was never idle and always worked in her various gardens. Poor eyesight, glaucoma, and a failing heart brought her to her knees and her passing in October 1968.
I shall not forget her as long as I live.

THREE COWS AND OUR REGISTERED BULL IN THE FIELD BELOW
COON DITCH LOOKING FOR A HANDOUT OF HAY

Spring 1987

The Rat Creek Fire of July 1985 burned just about everything above the highway. The area around the Old House did not burn and our strenuous efforts prevented our water tank, workshops, barn and house from burning as well. Many of the cattle were out on the range and some were badly burned, and others were killed by the fire. Approximately 30 survivors were kept in the fields below the highway and fed daily to keep their strength up. It was the following February before they could be let back out on the range.

The fire started from a lightning strike approximately four air miles from our ranch and took two days to advance down the Coast to us. It had to cross both Big Creek and Vicente Creek. It would creep and crawl all night then flare up violently each afternoon. High temperature, dry air and nearly limitless fuel made it one of the worst fires I had ever seen in the area.

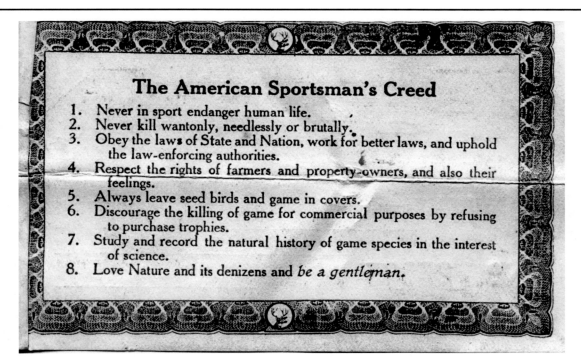

The American Sportsman's Creed

1. Never in sport endanger human life.
2. Never kill wantonly, needlessly or brutally.
3. Obey the laws of State and Nation, work for better laws, and uphold the law-enforcing authorities.
4. Respect the rights of farmers and property-owners, and also their feelings.
5. Always leave seed birds and game in covers.
6. Discourage the killing of game for commercial purposes by refusing to purchase trophies.
7. Study and record the natural history of game species in the interest of science.
8. Love Nature and its denizens and *be a gentleman.*

$1.00 · STATE OF CALIFORNIA · **$1.00**
HUNTING LICENSE

NOT TRANSFERABLE — CITIZEN — OBSERVE THE LAW

NAME Geo. W Harlan
AGE 29   HEIGHT 5-8
EYES COLOR Blue   HAIR COLOR Brown
RESIDENCE Fresno Cal

No. 25865   DATE ISSUED 4/30/21   OWNER'S SIGNATURE

EXPIRES JUNE 30, 1922

THE BACK AND FRONT OF MY FATHER'S DEER HUNTING LICENSE
FOR THE LICENSE YEAR 1921—1922

*George seldom hunted deer, but on occasion he killed one for protein in our diet.
We rarely killed the cash crop of a beef or pig.*

A REPRODUCTION OF A PAINTING OF OUR OLD BARN BEFORE ITS
DEMISE AT THE HARLAN RANCH

This is an example of how nature and disrespectful humanity bring old memories to a rapid close. This barn was very usable into the 1950's but it was misused by passing hippies who stayed overnight in the 60's. They removed the split side boards and used them for making a fire within the barn. It was an action very difficult to police by my father. He lived about ½ mile away and though he frequently did evict people from the barn, there were always those who came later in the evening and managed to complete their stay overnight. It eventually became a hazard to anyone entering because of the missing support members. So my father and Donald bulldozed it all into a pile where it could no longer cause injury and possible suit.

DONALD'S DOG, TERRY, IN A FIELD OF POPPIES AT THE HARLAN
RANCH AT LOPEZ POINT

Terry, born on July 4, 1999, was acquired by Donald as a puppy. He is a pure bred Giant Rat Terrier and spent his first five years on the ranch until Donald's death in August of 2004. Stanley took over his care at that point and regularly visited the ranch until 2007 when the ranch was sold.

He is not a cattle dog but does his thing with cows and calves as he sees fit. He is very fast on his feet and was observed outrunning a young coyote which he ran into and barreled over. He had a close encounter with a mountain lion near the ranch house one night and received a 4-inch scratch on his shoulder. He now enjoys a much quieter life with Stanley and Irene in Monterey with only occasional visits with neighborhood raccoons.

THE HARLAN RANCH LOOKING UP THE HILL IN A NORTH NORTHEAST DIRECTION FROM LOPEZ POINT

This view of the ranch is somewhat unusual in that it was observed from near the ocean bank at Lopez Point looking up the hill. Only the southeast portion of the ranch shows in this picture but most of what is seen is a part of the Harlan Ranch.

This scene represents a beautiful time of the year when the grass is green and the animals well fed. Sometimes the rains come early in the fall and this scene can be observed even before Christmas. On a more typical year the rains come in mid-winter and spring and the grass greens up only after the weather warms somewhat. This photo was taken on April 6, 2006.

A GROUP OF CONTENTED YOUNG CATTLE GRAZING IN THE HARLAN FIELDS

April 6, 2006

This group of weaned calves was the last to graze in the Harlan fields. They belonged to the Packard family and the Miltons and were pastured here during their weaning period.

After Donald's death it was very difficult for the family to maintain the ranch as it had been and, at the same time, take care of their other responsibilities. The Harlan cattle were sold and our good neighbors were encouraged to graze their animals on our land as we had done on theirs before Donald's death. George and Esther would have done the same, I am sure.

HARLAN ROCK SOUTH OF POINT "16"

Circa 1987

Most official maps of the area include this Harlan namesake. It is somewhat obscure compared to Lopez Rock or even some of the unnamed offshore rocks in the area. It is not known who named it initially.

TERRY PRACTICING HIS POSE NEAR THE CATTLE GUARD
BY THE RANCH HOUSE

March 4, 2006

Terry seems to be a regular ham when it comes to photography. Ever since I have taken over Terry's care after Donald's passing he seems to recognize that he is on camera and will hold a pose for and extended period of time. Through very little encouragement on my part he took on this stance at the end of the rock wall above the end of the cattle guard.

He follows basic commands quite well but has not shown any great wisdom when it comes to learning new tricks. Donald got him as a puppy and served his master well for those first five years. Donald proclaimed that Terry was his ears and eyes in being aware of his surroundings.

TERRY LOOKING WISTFULLY OUT TOWARD LOPEZ ROCK FROM
THE STONE SUPPORTING DONALD'S PLAQUE—

March 18, 2007

This rock, embedded in the soil of our northwest field, was chosen as the spot for mounting Donald's plaque. He had stated he wanted his ashes to be buried in the same location where the native Indians had buried their dead.

In the 1930's George Harlan developed a spring in the Ranchito watershed and installed piping for irrigating the northwest portion of our fields. In digging the trenches for laying the pipe Indian bones were found in this area. It had also been a favorite campsite for those Indians who lived along the Lopez Point coastline. Black soil, sea shells, flint pieces, arrow heads, mortars and pestles were a signature of their earlier presence.

SUNSET AT LOPEZ POINT

February 11, 2006

One of the rewards of living at Lopez Point was to view the variable and sometimes spectacular sunsets. This one shows winter storm clouds concealing the direct light of the sun, but also the spectacular backlighting of the cloud's irregular shapes.

Close inspection of the horizon reveals a tug boat pulling two loaded lumber barges from the northwest forests to the populated areas of southern California. This method of moving large quantities of lumber was developed after World War II. Previous methods were to ship by lumber schooners which plied the coastal waters much closer to shore. A favorite past time of my grandmother was to sit on the front porch of our old home and watch the various ships pass by. On some occasions they were close enough to read the name on the bow of the ship.

UNIQUE ROCK SHOWING WHERE A WATER COURSE HAD
ERODED IT AT SOME TIME IN PAST HISTORY

June 19, 2007

This sandstone type formation was imbedded in the cliff face of the big flat for untold centuries. The back side was exposed during my lifetime and simply appeared to be a large rounded rock hanging precipitously in the cliff face approximately 80 feet above the beach level. After the turn of the century sufficient support gave way around its edges and it fell to the beach level. What had been hidden from sight was this now exposed surface showing a deeply eroded face that had at some time been directly in a watercourse. The nearest similar stone can be found on the eastern side of the mountain top possibly 4 miles distant. It can be assumed that a massive wash occurred in these mountains at some time in the past, forming the fields that are a part of the Harlan Ranch and Lopez Point.

STATE OF CALIFORNIA

THE BOARD OF EDUCATION OF _Monterey_ COUNTY

AWARDS THIS

DIPLOMA OF GRADUATION

FROM THE EIGHTH GRADE

TO _Stanley Vernon Harlan_

FOR HAVING COMPLETED THE ELEMENTARY SCHOOL COURSE OF STUDY IN

THE _Redwood Branch_ ELEMENTARY SCHOOL DISTRICT

AWARDED _June 30th_ 19_41_

W. H. Reed PRESIDENT

Jas. G. Force SECRETARY

STANLEY'S GRADUATION DIPLOMA FROM REDWOOD BRANCH ELEMENTARY SCHOOL—DATED JUNE 30, 1941

I have included this photographic reproduction of my graduation diploma for a number of reasons. I was the last student to graduate from this school before its closure in 1942. My mother was my only teacher from 1st through 8th grade. My father was a primary mover of our elementary education in that he built this school that I attended for the last four years with his bare hands and a few basic carpentry tools. My mother held all of her students to very high personal character and educational standards. Of the six students she taught in the 1936-1937 school year four of them went on to graduate from college and were very successful in their chosen fields. I attribute any successes I may have had to her excellence of teaching.

A HARLAN COW 20 HOURS AFTER THE RAT CREEK FIREPASSED
THROUGH THE AREA OF SECTION 8, T 22S, R 4 E

My father, George Harlan, after a ranch auto accident, was in a comma at a local rest home on this day in July of 1985. His herd of range cattle had been decimated by the Rat Creek Fire of 1985. Started by a lightning strike a number of miles away the fire was allowed to advance in all directions over a period of three days. "We should let naturally caused fires burn themselves out" was the quote from Forest Service management. This scene, unpleasant as it is, is just one consequence of letting a fire rage through tinder dry conditions in areas where fuels have been allowed to accumulate for many years due to lack of controlled burns at times of the year when only limited areas will burn.

Pioneer homestead houses in the area had survived for over 80 years until this fateful time in 1985 when all were lost. Historically tragic, humanely tragic and an outright disgrace to forest management is the only way to describe it.

THIS SCENE IS THE UDDER OF "CRISP" A "SURVIVOR" OF THE
RAT CREEK FIRE OF 1985--45 DAYS AFTER THE FIRE

Of a herd of 40 animals my father lost 5 outright and 5 more succumbed to their injuries soon after. This cow seriously burned over most of her body, survived, but was no longer able to nurse and consequently was sent to the slaughter house a few months later.

My brother, Donald, nursed a number of the herd back to health by individual feeding and daily care. He appropriately gave this animal a new name, "Crisp".

County, State and Federal controls have literally put the coastal ranchers out of business. Where my father grazed nearly 200 head of cattle none are there now

THIS LARGE 3 POINT BUCK WAS ONE OF MANY WHO WERE
CASUALTIES OF THE RAT CREEK FIRE

July 1985

On this day, 20 hours after the fire has passed over, I counted 5 dead cows and more than 20 dead deer in a relatively small area of Section 8, Township 22 south and Range 4 east. Most of the deer were caught in their day beds and didn't even make an effort to get up or run from the advancing fire. I observed one on a bare patch of ground that had not been burned at all but yet lay dead as if it had been poisoned by an advancing carbon monoxide cloud.

A flock of nearly 100 crows which inhabited the area for as long as anyone can remember were wiped out. To this day, 25 years later, not one has returned.

A VIEW UP OUR CANYON AT THE RANCH A FEW MONTHS AFTER THE RAT CREEK FIRE OF 1985

The ashes had settled, the rains had come and green grass was appearing on the burned ground. The redwood trees still show signs of their burning to their crowns and the side hill across the creek show signs of having been burned to the bare ground.

The white guest house and Stanley's work shop are no longer there. Both were lost to the fire. Donald's and Stanley's efforts to save the main house, the barn, the water tank and some of the outbuildings were successful. However, when we rebuilt the workshop after the fire the County red tagged our efforts and placed our equity of the complete ranch in jeopardy until they were paid a planning fee. Incidentally, the property taxes on the ranch increased the maximum allowed by law that year as well.

Made in the USA
Lexington, KY
13 November 2018